# 10th Grade All Subjects Workbook

Beyond Books
Learning Resources

Copyright © Kay Cauler

All rights reserved. This book or any portion thereof may not be reproduced or used in any manner whatsoever without the express written permission of the publisher.

First printing, 2024

| | |
|---|---|
| *MATH* | *1* |
| *VOCABULARY* | *17* |
| *WRITING* | *45* |
| *HISTORY* | *79* |
| *SCIENCE* | *124* |
| *SOLUTIONS* | *154* |

BEYONDBOOKSLEARNING.COM

Visit beyondbookslearning.com for more resources and to learn about our mission!

# Happy with your purchase?

Please leave a review! Your reviews help our small business grow and create more effective workbooks! Thank you!

Concerns? Leave us a message at beyondbookslearning.com.
We are unable to reply to you on Amazon.

# U.S.A.

# Math

# Important Formulas

## Quadratic Formula:

What are quadratics? A quadratic is a mathematical expression of more than two algebraic terms where there is a minimum of one term that is squared, but no terms have a higher degree than 2. Three types of quadratic equations:

**Standard form:**

$y = ax^2 + bx + c$

**Factored form:**

$y = a(x - r_1)(x - r_2)$

**Vertex form:**

$y = a(x - h)^2 + k$

**The quadratic Formula:**

This formula is used to find the solutions of a quadratic equation where $a \neq 0$.

$(-b \pm \sqrt{(b^2 - 4ac)}) / (2a)$

## Slope-Intercept Form:

This is a linear equation representing a line on a coordinate plane where m is the slope and b is the y intercept.

$y = mx + b$

## Pythagorean Theorem:

Used to solve problems involving right triangles where a and b are legs and c is the hypotenuse.

$a^2 + b^2 = c^2$

**1.** Find the hypotenuse of the right triangle.

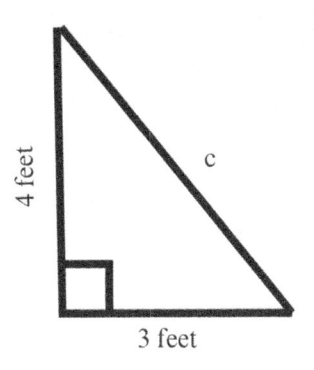

*4 feet* / *c* / *3 feet*

**2.** A triangle has angles in the ratio 1 : 2 : 3. Find the measure of each angle.

**3.** Find the missing length of the right triangle.

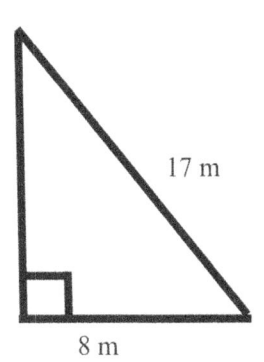

*17 m* / *8 m*

**Triangles**

4. A ladder is leaning against a wall with its base 12 feet away from the wall, making a 45° angle with the ground. What is the length of the ladder?

5. Triangle ABC has sides AB = 8 meters, BC = 10 meters, and AC = 6 meters. Determined whether or not triangle ABC is a right triangle.

6. In triangle ABC, angle A is 45°, angle B in 65°, and angle C is 70°. Is the triangle acute, right, or obtuse? Why?

7. A tower casts a shadow on the ground that is 4 yards long when the angle of elevation of the sun is 55°. What is the height of the tower, given it is perpendicular to the ground?

**Triangles**

**8.** A regular polygon has an exterior angle of 30°. How many sides does it have?

**9.** A regular polygon has an exterior angle of 90°. How many sides does it have?

**10.** You want to purchase two goats to start your goat milk soap business. Your local ordinance requires a minimum pen area of 15 ft² per goat. Your available land will require the pen to be a rectangular shape. What are the minimum dimensions of one rectangular pen for both goats?

**11.** You decide to build the pen from problem 10 in the dimensions 6 feet × 5 feet. How many feet of fencing will you need to build the fence?

**Polygons**

**12.** You have a flower bed that measures 5 feet × 4 feet. You want to cover the flower bed in 2 inches of mulch. The mulch is sold in bags that each cover 2 cubic feet. How many bags will you need to buy?

**13.** Your friend asks you to help with placing wallpaper in her study. The shape of the wall is a trapezoid with the length of the two horizontal parallel sides being 3 meters and 5.5 meters. The height is 3 meters. Find the area of the wall so you know how much wallpaper is needed.

**14.** Luke wants to design a sticker for his laptop. It will be a pentagon with each side being 8 cm long. What is the perimeter of the sticker?

**Polygons**

**15.** Solve the quadratic equation $x^2 + 4x + 5 = 0$

**16.** Solve the quadratic equation $x^2 + 2x + 2 = 4$

**17.** Solve the quadratic equation by factoring $x^2 - 5x + 6 = 0$

**18.** Solve the quadratic equation by completing the square $x^2 + 6x - 3 = 0$

**Quadratic Equations**

**19.** Solve using substitution
$x + y = 5$
$2x - y = 7$




**20.** Solve using substitution
$x + y = 7$
$x - y = 3$




**21.** Solve using substitution
$2x + y = 10$
$x - 3y = 5$

**Systems of Equations**

**22.** Solve using elimination
2x + 3y = 15
x - 3y = 3




**23.** Solve using elimination
2x + 3y = 6
x + 2y = 5




**24.** Solve using elimination
2x + 3y = 8
4x + 3y = -2

**Systems of Equations**

**25.** Solve the inequality 3x -5 ≥ 10 for x and plot the solutions on the number line.

**26.** Solve the inequality 6x + 12 < 4x - 10 for x and plot the solutions on the number line.

**27.** Graph the solution set for the following inequality on the number line -6 < x < 4.

**28.** Write the inequality that matches the solution depicted on the number line.

**Inequalities**

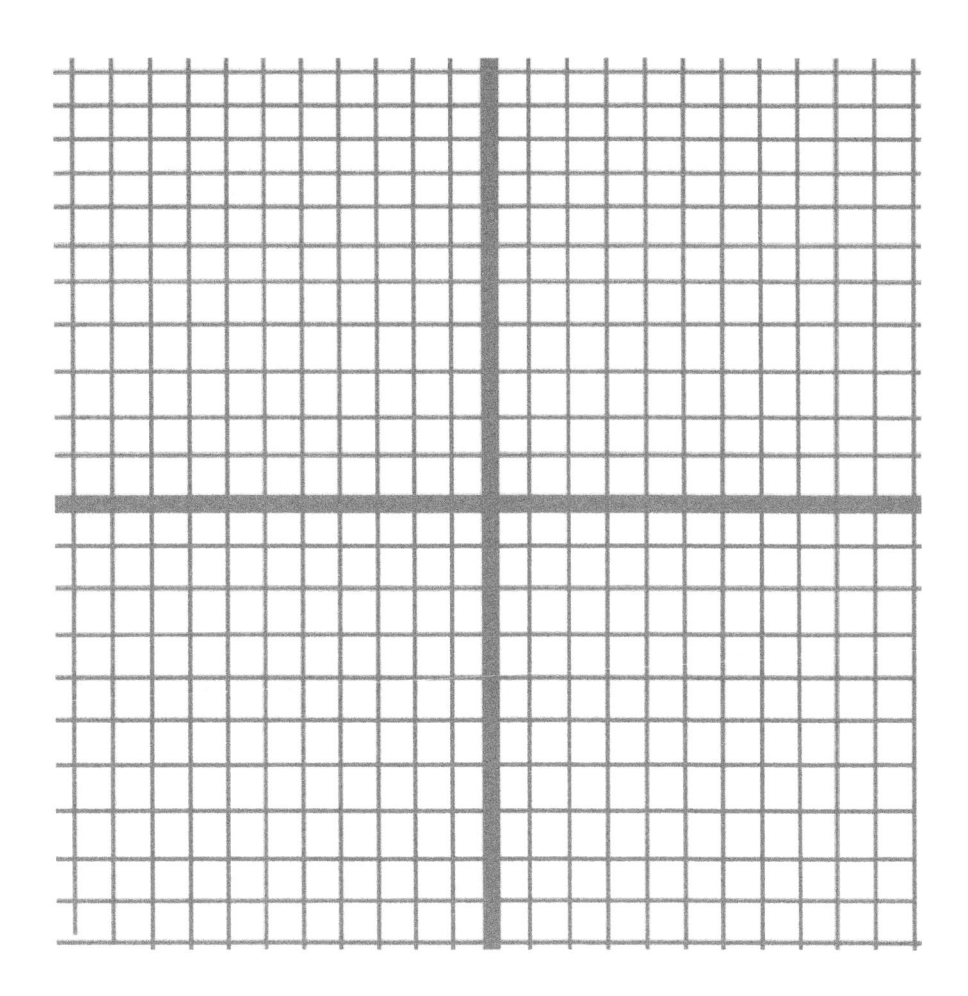

**29.** Find the slope and y intercept then graph: y = 3x + 5

**30.** Find the slope-intercept form of the equation of a line that passes through the coordinates, (3,0) and (0,6).

**Graphing**

**31.** Given the quadratic function f(x) = $x^2$ + 4x - 5 find the vertex, axis of symmetry, and whether the parabola opens upward or downward.

**32.** Given the quadratic function f(x) = -$x^2$ + 2x + 3 find the vertex, axis of symmetry, and whether the parabola opens upward or downward.

**33.** Is there a scenario where the parabola of a quadratic function would open to the left or right instead of up or down?

**Quadratic Functions**

**34.** Suppose your business's social media account sends out a viral video. The views double every 8 hours. Write a logarithmic equation to represent the amount of video views over time. Then determine how long it will take to reach 1 million views if you start with 200.

**35.** Find the value of x in $\log_2(x) = 3$

**36.** In your own words, explain logarithms. What practical applications do they have?

**Logarithms**

**37.** If the length of a rectangle is half its width and the perimeter is 16 cm, what are the dimensions of the rectangle?

**38.** A car drives a constant speed of 65 km/h. If it travels for 3.5 hours, how far will it travel?

**39.** Your friend wants to know how long it would take to drive from your house to your vacation home for a weekend trip. If the distance between the two houses is 465 miles and you drive at an average speed of 55 miles an hour, how long will it take to get there? What time should you leave to get there by 4pm with a one hour lunch stop?

**Word Problems**

**40.** If you drive your car at a constant speed (s) for 48 minutes and travel a distance of 55 km, how fast were you traveling in km/h?

**41.** Allen wants to save for a new phone. The phone he wants costs $850. Allen works a part-time job making $13 an hour after tax. If he works 17 hours/ week, how many weeks will it take him to save for the phone if he doesn't spend his money on anything else?

**42.** Ella wants to tile her bathroom floor. The bathroom is 8 feet × 6 feet. If each tile is 6 inches × 6 inches, how many tiles will she need to finish the floor?

**Word Problems**

**43.** Jack notices a tree in his yard casts a shadow 5 meters long at the same time of day his shadow is 3 meters long. If Jack is 2 meters tall, how tall is the tree?

**44.** You decide you would like to buy a new television. You see two local stores running sales on the same t.v. Store A is selling the t.v. for $700 with a 15% discount. Store B is selling it for $650 with a 10% discount. Which is the better deal?

**45.** You and your friends are planning a group trip to see a play. There are 7 of you altogether. The trip will cost a total of $866 for gas and lodging plus $115 per ticket. What should each person pay to divide the cost evenly?

**Word Problems**

# Vocabulary

**Define each word using your favorite dictionary or dictionary website. Make sure to note the part of speech (i.e. verb, noun, adjective, etc.).**

**Acquiesce:** (verb) accept something without protest

**Aesthetic:** (adjective) concerned with beauty or the appreciation of beauty

**Alacrity:** (noun) brisk and cheerful readiness

**Aplomb:** (noun) self-confidence or assurance, especially when in a demanding situation

**Aristocrat:** (noun) a member of the aristocracy

**Articulate:** (adjective) having or showing the ability to speak fluently and coherently.

**Assimilate:** (verb) take in and understand fully, info or ideas

**Define** 8·26·24

# Use the vocabulary words in a sentence.

He acquiesced when they told him to eat dessert.

She didn't like the lamp because it wasn't aesthetic.

I ate the cookie dough with alacrity.

They were aplomb after their first babysitting job.

Marquis de Lafayette was an aristocrat.

She was able to articulate wonderfully in the rough debate.

He struggled to assimilate the science homework.

8·26·24

**Define each word using your favorite dictionary or dictionary website. Make sure to note the part of speech (i.e. verb, noun, adjective, etc.).**

**Begrudge:** (verb) give reluctantly or resentfully

**Benevolent:** (adjective) kind and with positive intentions

**Capitulate:** (verb) cease to resist an opponent or an unwelcomed demand; yield

**Chaff:** (noun) worthless things; rubbish

**Chagrin:** (noun) annoyance or distress at having failed or been humiliated

**Complacency:** (noun) a feeling of smug or uncritical satisfaction with oneself or one's achievements

**Composite:** (verb) combine (2 or more images) to make a single picture.
(noun) a thing made up of several parts or elements.

**Define** 8·26·24

# Use the vocabulary words in a sentence.

She begrudges giving her phone charger to her sister.

The cat looked benevolent when she bit me.

I had to capitulate to my mother's hug.

The healthy protein bars tasted like they were chaff.

His chagrin was being shorter than his sister.

You weren't bad, but you shouldn't have complacency.

This collage is a composite of things I've saved for years.

8·26·24

**Example Sentences**

**Define each word using your favorite dictionary or dictionary website. Make sure to note the part of speech (i.e. verb, noun, adjective, etc.).**

**Conviction:** (noun) a firmly held belief or opinion

**Cynical:** (adjective) believing that people are motivated purely by self-interest; distrustful of human sincerity or integrity

**Daft:** (adjective) silly, foolish, or eccentric

**Debilitate:** (verb) make someone weak and infirm

**Democracy:** (noun) a system of government by the whole population or all the eligible members of a state, typically through elected representatives.

**Devoid:** (adjective) entirely lacking or free from

**Dredge:** (verb) bring up or clear something from a river or body of water, or bring up something unwelcome and forgotten or obscure to people's attention

**Define**

# Use the vocabulary words in a sentence.

I had a conviction that the cookie did not vanish into thin air.

Stop being cynical.

Don't be so daft.

The lack of sleep made him debilitate.

America is a democracy.

Her voice was devoid of excitement.

I didn't like that he dredges up that one story.

**Define each word using your favorite dictionary or dictionary website. Make sure to note the part of speech (i.e. verb, noun, adjective, etc.).**

**Edify:** (verb) instruct or improve (someone) morally or intellectually.

**Elucidate:** (verb) make something clear.

**Enmity:** (noun) the state or feeling of being actively opposed or hostile to someone or something.

**Fascism:** (noun) an authoritarian and nationalistic right-winged system of government and social organization

**Feasible:** (adjective) possible to do easily or conveniently

**Frivolous:** (adjective) not having any serious purpose or value.

**Furtive:** (adjective) attempting to avoid notice or attention

**Define**

# Use the vocabulary words in a sentence.

Her comments had not helped edify their doubts and questions.

Their hand gestures weren't useful to elucidate.

After the fall there was enmity between God and man.

Hitler's killing of the Jews was fascism.

It is not feasible to go shopping with toddlers.

She made a lot of frivolous purchases.

They looked furtive, refusing to look at the broken vase.

**Example Sentences**

9·13·24

**Define each word using your favorite dictionary or dictionary website. Make sure to note the part of speech (i.e. verb, noun, adjective, etc.).**

**Gaudy:** (adjective) extravagantly bright or showy, typically so as to be tasteless.

**Gist:** (noun) the substance or essence of a speech or text.

**Hyperbole:** (noun) exaggerated statements or claims not meant to be taken literally.

**Hypothetical:** (adjective) supposed but not necessarily real or true.

**Implication:** (noun) the conclusion that can be drawn from something although it's not explicitly stated

**Incredulous:** (adjective) unwilling or unable to believe something

**Ineffable:** (adjective) too great or extreme to be expressed or described in words.

**Define**

# Use the vocabulary words in a sentence.

The holiday decoration was excessively gaudy.

Though I wasn't paying attention, I think I got the gist of it.

Grandma often speaks in hyperboles.

Hypothetically, a house cat could kill you in your sleep.

There was strong implication about house chores when we got home

She seemed incredulous that I didn't want to pet the beetle.

God is ineffable.

**Define each word using your favorite dictionary or dictionary website. Make sure to note the part of speech (i.e. verb, noun, adjective, etc.).**

Introspection:

Jeopardize:

Jurisdiction:

Kin:

Levity:

Morose:

Myriad:

**Define**

# Use the vocabulary words in a sentence.

**Example Sentences**

**Define each word using your favorite dictionary or dictionary website. Make sure to note the part of speech (i.e. verb, noun, adjective, etc.).**

**Negligent:**

**Niche:**

**Nonchalant:**

**Oblique:**

**Ominous:**

**Pallor:**

**Proponent:**

**Define**

# Use the vocabulary words in a sentence.

**Example Sentences**

**Define each word using your favorite dictionary or dictionary website. Make sure to note the part of speech (i.e. verb, noun, adjective, etc.).**

**Prune:**

**Publican:**

**Quell:**

**Rapport:**

**Rebuke:**

**Reconcile:**

sanctity:

**Define**

# Use the vocabulary words in a sentence.

**Example Sentences**

**Define each word using your favorite dictionary or dictionary website. Make sure to note the part of speech (i.e. verb, noun, adjective, etc.).**

Scorn:

Serendipity:

Stolid:

Succinct:

Sumptuous:

Specemen:

Tacit:

**Define**

# Use the vocabulary words in a sentence.

**Example Sentences**

**Define each word using your favorite dictionary or dictionary website. Make sure to note the part of speech (i.e. verb, noun, adjective, etc.).**

**Teem:**

**Tenuous:**

**Trajectory:**

**Tyranny:**

**Unobtrusive:**

**Valid:**

**Vapid:**

**Define**

# Use the vocabulary words in a sentence.

**Example Sentences**

# Choose 4 of the previous vocabulary words to depict in a sketch.

**Sketches**

**Create a poem or short story that includes at least 5 of the previous vocabulary words. Be creative and use them in context to display understanding of the meaning.**

**Creative Writing**

**Creative Writing**

Create a commercial ad using 5 vocabulary words from the list.

**Choose one of the vocabulary words previously defined and create a collage from magazine clippings, printed pictures, stickers, etc. that exemplifies the essence of the word.**

**Vocab Collage**

**Choose a movie, show, or book you have recently watched/read. Write a review using as many vocabulary words as possible while still making sense. Don't be afraid to get creative!**

**Write a Review**

Create an article for a fictional newspaper in your town about an exciting upcoming event. Be as creative as you'd like. Include 3 vocabulary words.

**Write an Argument**

# Writing

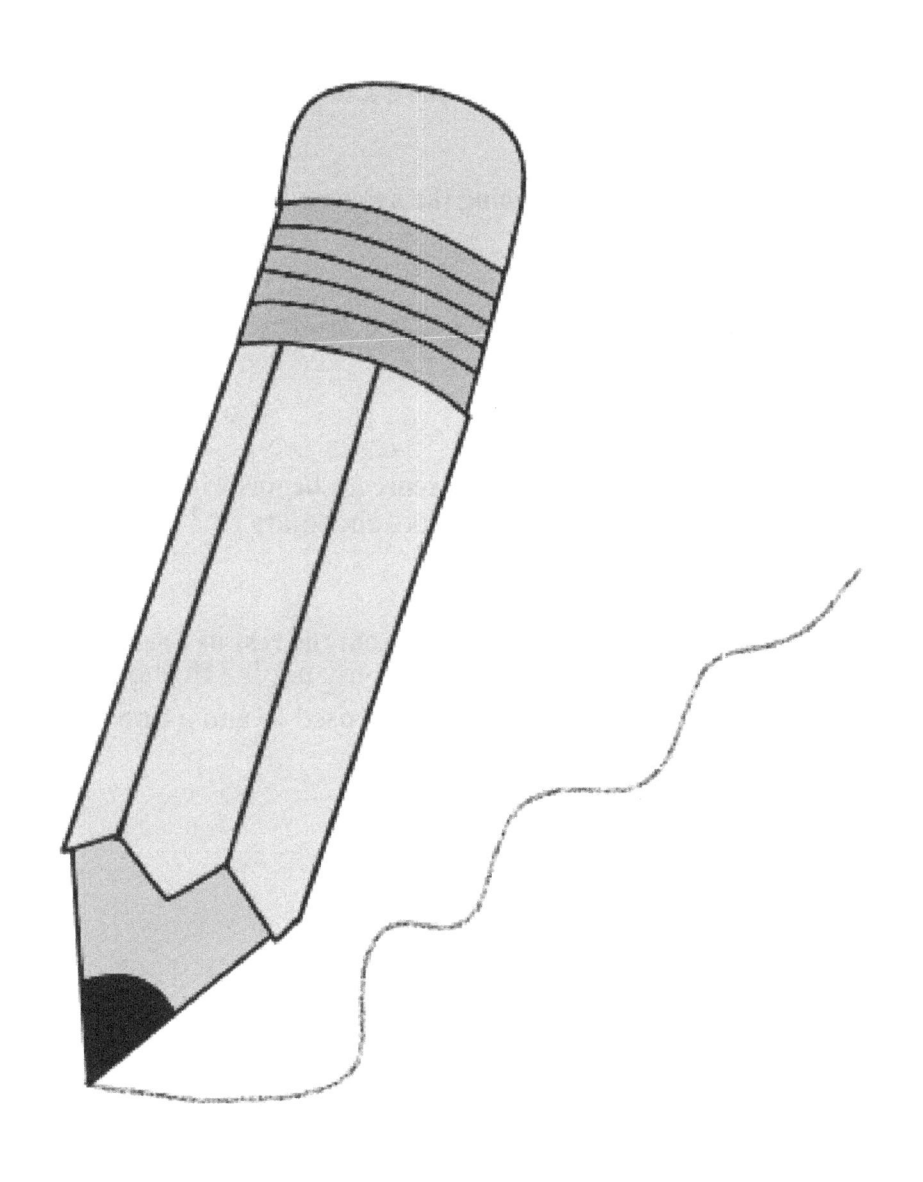

# Tips for Comma Usage

**After a dependent clause that starts a sentence**
When she rode her bike, she broke her arm.

**Between contrasting elements**
The man was old, not young.

**Between items in a series**
The dog chewed the shoe, the toy, and the chair leg.

**Before the conjunction connecting independent clauses**
I had fun at the beach, but I should have worn a hat to protect my skin.

**Between two or more adjectives describing the same noun**
The woman drove an old, broken car.

**When writing dates and locations**
July 4, 1776          London, England

**After an introductory word or phrase or if a sentence begins with a freestanding "yes" or "no"**
First, I need to make my bed.   No, I don't like chocolate.

**Before a quotation or to seperate a quoatation from the rest of a sentence**
The boy said, "That's my book."   OR   "That's my book," the boy said. (Note: an exclamation point or question mark may also be used to end a quotation in the middle of a sentence.)

**Before and after an interrupter**
The girl, who had studied all weekend, aced her test.

**Before and after an introduction**
My sister, Barbara, has never flown in an airplane.

**When directly addressing someone**
Jason, clean your room!

**Comma Usage Rules**

# Parts of Speech

**Adjective**
A word that modifies or describes a noun or pronoun
colors, heights, tastes, smells, size, etc.

**Adverb**
Words describing how many, how often, when, and where. These words are used to describe an adjective, adverb, or verb.

**Conjunction**
Joins words, phrases, or clauses
Examples: "and, because, but, therefore, so," etc.

**Interjection**
Words that express strong emotions or feelings
"Wow, Oh, Ouch," etc.
Interjections can also be used to give a command or address someone

**Noun**
A person, place, thing, or idea

**Preposition**
Words that show place, time, or direction such as "on, in, at, above, about, from," etc.

**Pronoun**
Words that can be used to replace a noun such as "he, her, you, me," etc.

**Verb**
Words showing action or a state of being
"jump, sleep, read, am, is, were, had," etc.

# Persuasive Writing

**What is persuasive writing?**
Persuasive writing is a type of writing meant to convince the reader of a certain belief or idea. We encounter this type of writing on a regular basis in our daily lives. If we can understand the goal of persuasive writing and how it is constructed, we can identify and understand it.

Commonly, persuasive writing is used in advertising with the goal of convincing you that you have a need that only the advertised product can fill. Another tactic in marketing is the use of the reviews. These are often persuasive in nature. The reviewer usually relates why they believe you should or should not buy the product. Incorporating good reviews in ads helps persuade you to buy.

Many speeches are written to persuade or convince the listeners of something. They sell people, promises, or ideas.

**What are the key elements and strategies of persuasive writing?**

### A clear Thesis statement

A thesis statement is the argument or point you are trying to make. Your entire persuasive piece will be centered around this idea or opinion. Because a thesis statement is essentially an opinion, it will almost always be of a controversial nature. The thesis statement must be clearly defined and works as the backbone of the entire persuasive work. Each paragraph and point of the paper must support this thesis or the paper becomes weak. Alternate opinions should be raised and dismantled to create a stronger point.

### Writing for the Audience

In order to effectively reach the audience so they will abandon their current beliefs and opinions to adopt yours, you must understand them, their interests, and the way they think. Understanding this aspect of writing will transform the very language choices you make. There are three specific tones used in persuasive writing: ethos, logos, and pothos.

### Ethos or Character

This is the concept of credibility in the writer. Credibility is essential to persuasive writing, because the more credibility you have (especially in the topic in question), the more likely your reader is to take your opinions into consideration. The reader needs to feel the writer has more knowledge, experience, or expertise in the matter than s/he does to take your argument seriously. Essentially, the writer is trustworthy enough to listen to.

### Logos or Logic

Logos is the form of writing that appeals to the logical side of the reader. This is where the writer will use statistics, facts, expert interpretations, and logical reasoning to build credibility and convince the reader of the validity of his/her opinion.

**Persuasive Writing Tips**

## Pothos or Emotion

Evoking feelings in the reader is a very common and effective strategy. Think about how many advertisements appeal to some emotion to get you to buy a product. Making someone feel sentimental is a good way to get them to buy a gift for a friend or loved one.
In political speeches, the speaker will often address matters they know will ignite a fire of intense feeling in their listener, and then they will promise to fix the issue and/or describe how their opponent has caused the issue. The use of specific language is critical to this form of persuasion.

## Counterarguments

You might think addressing alternate ideas would hurt your argument, but it is actually not the case. In fact, ignoring well-known arguments is actually more harmful than not. Assume your reader is well-informed enough to know the popular ideas surrounding the topic, which is why they have interest in reading your thoughts in the first place. If your writing shows a lack of experience or knowledge about common beliefs, your readers will pick up on this quickly. It becomes your burden to effectively and tactfully refute the opposition. Not only does it help present you as open to ideas, but it shows you have critical thinking skills - you are aware of the other options and have thoughtfully considered them, still concluding your opinion is best.

## Grab Their Attention and Keep It

Your introduction must grab the attention of the reader, but the rest of your paper must keep it. Understanding pacing is important to retaining the interest of the reader. Your thesis should be clear enough that the reader knows exactly what to expect in your paper, and then you must deliver it. Make sure all points lead to your thesis. Then, you must wrap the entire paper up in a neat little bow that is the concluding paragraph. The conclusion should summarize key points, reiterate the thesis, and leave a lasting impression or call-to-action for the reader. A call-to-action is an action you call on the reader to complete in the name of your cause which places power in the reader's hands to change something in his/her life or lives of others.

## Language and Tone

We mentioned the importance of choice of language earlier. The ultimate goal of a persuasive writer is to use the most vivid language possible. You want to implement strong imagery so your reader is as close to the topic, in mind and emotion, as possible. Common persuasive techniques include repetition, rhetorical questions, and parallelism. The goal is to captivate the reader's attention, fully. The tone of the paper should always remain confident but respectful.

## Logical Organization

A key factor in writing persuasively is to keep all content well organized. Make sure the evidence is planned out and written in an order that is easy to follow and flows well. If the reader becomes confused or feels like your thoughts are jumbled, he/she may abandon your views and dismiss them as unevolved or half-baked. Keep the reading flow on-track and smooth.

# Steps to Build a Persuasive Argument

**Choose a Topic and Clear Position**
The first step is to choose a topic and then decide what your position is on that topic. This must be a very clear position with little to no "gray" areas. An effective persuasive piece is very firm and clear. Your position should be assertive and have an element of controversy so it can be debated. In this way, your argument may be compelling enough to consider.

**Do Your Research**
It is important to be well-informed on your topic. Nothing will squash your credibility more than being ill-informed. You must know a wide range of facts, statistics, and information surrounding the topic *as well as* counter positions and alternative thoughts and ideas. It is important to not only research credible authorities on the subject, websites, expert opinions, studies, etc. but also gauge what common people are saying and believe inside the arena of the topic. These people could be influencers of some sort who share in spreading their ideas and beliefs even if they are not well-founded.

**Get to Know Your Audience**
Who are the people you will be appealing to? Who is going to care about this paper? What are their core values, current beliefs, interests, etc.? Identify them as precisely as possible so you can construct a piece that will speak directly to them in a language that addresses their interests, concerns, and emotions using language and examples that resonate with them. Speak to your audience in a way that reassures them you know what matters most to them, and connect with them in this way.

**Develop a Solid Thesis Statement**
Craft a clear and assertive thesis statement that concisely conveys your position on the subject. Your thesis should tell the reader exactly what to expect to find inside your writing.

**Outline**
Build an outline that organizes all the main points and supporting details in a logical, flowing manner. Start with an introduction that captures your reader's attention and presents your thesis statement. The body of the work comes next. Each paragraph should focus on its own supporting point with related evidence. Then, the conclusion should reinforce all the main supporting points of the paper as well as reiterate the thesis and leave the reader with a firm sense of confidence in your point and, possibly, a call-to-action.

**Persuasive Writing Tips**

On the following pages, you will be given persuasive writing prompts. Use the lined pages provided to collect evidence, form a thesis, or outline your work. When you are finished with each assignment, read it to a fellow human to get feedback. Becoming a strong persuasive writer takes plenty of practice and constructive criticism from listeners. Also, reading the finished product out loud allows you to hear the flow in a way a second reader might hear it. You may notice areas that need changed, words that have been repeated, ideas that haven't been fully developed, etc.

Try using feedback from others positively to improve this incredible craft. Persuasive writing is a learned skill that takes practice to perfect. Eventually, you will find a persuasive voice and style that fits you.

**Remember ...**

- Use the persuasive techniques we learned. Employ logos, pothos, and/or ethos as well as a confident and respectful tone. Also use the persuasive language we spoke of.
- Write for your audience
- Address counterarguments
- Provide evidence, relatable examples, facts, and anecdotes
- Create a solid structure that makes your argument easy to track
- Leave a lasting impression with a persuasive conclusion

# Is social media a positive or negative influence for teenagers and young adults?

**Topics to consider ...**

- Socialization and connectivity
- Mental health
- Expanding ideas
- Inaccurate portrayals of reality
- Emotional and mental maturity
- Bullying
- Misinformation
- Organizing efforts and finding like-minded people
- Safety
- Data concerns

**Persuasive Writing Prompt**

**Make an argument against implementing school uniforms in public schools.**

**Topics to consider ...**

- Autonomy
- Self-expression
- Modesty
- Equality and peer pressure
- Focus on education
- Safety
- School pride
- Cost concerns
- Comfort
- Cultural and religious considerations

**Persuasive Writing Prompt**

**Now, make an argument for implementing school uniforms in public schools.**

**Persuasive Writing Prompt**

# Should standardized testing be used to evaluate student performance?

**Topics to consider ...**

- Teaching to test
- Objective measurements?
- Accountability of teachers and schools
- Data for decision-making
- Benchmarking
- Use by college admissions
- Stress and anxiety to students
- Limits of testing
- Disadvantaged groups
- Resource allocation

**Persuasive Writing Prompt**

**Create an argument for whether or not you believe volunteer work should be a requirement for high school graduation.**

**Topics to consider ...**

- Character development opportunities
- Civic engagement of students and the community
- Skill building
- College applications
- Exposure to new experiences
- Time constraints
- Turning otherwise rewarding experiences into compulsory work
- Access to opportunities
- Quality of services
- Administrative burden

**Persuasive Writing Prompt**

**You recently found a time machine. Persuade your parents to allow you to use it.**

**Topics to consider ...**

- Educational opportunities
- Preventing mistakes
- Changing history
- Family heritage
- Economic benefits
- Personal growth
- Adventures

**Persuasive Writing Prompt**

# Should the voting age be raised to 21 years?

**Topics to consider ...**

- Maturity
- Life experience
- Education and awareness
- Financial independence
- Civic engagement
- Legal responsibilities

**Persuasive Writing Prompt**

**Make an argument for or against implementing the use of robots as high school teachers.**

**Topics to consider ...**

- Reliability
- Personal learning
- Access to information
- Efficiency
- Cost
- Emotional intelligence capabilities
- Human connection
- Ethics
- Security

**Persuasive Writing Prompt**

# Make an argument for or against free college for everyone.

**Topics to consider ...**

- Equality
- Economic growth
- Debt reduction for students
- Increased enrollment
- Taxes
- Quality concerns
- Value of education and degrees

**Persuasive Writing Prompt**

# Should mental health education be mandatory in high school?

**Topics to consider ...**

- Early intervention
- Support
- Awareness and stigma reduction
- Coping skills
- Resource allocation
- Curriculum overload
- Privacy
- Effectiveness
- Parental support

**Persuasive Writing Prompt**

**Argue whether or not you believe Big Foot exists.**

**Topics to consider ...**

- Eyewitness accounts
- Footprints and physical evidence
- Historical references and legends
- Audio recordings
- Photographic and video evidence
- Hoaxes
- Scientific community consensus
- Misidentification

**Persuasive Writing Prompt**

## Should the work week be changed to 4 days?

**Topics to consider ...**

- Work - life balance
- Productivity
- Health and wellness
- Environmental impacts
- Employee satisfaction and retention
- Operational challenges
- GDP
- Consumer expectations
- Transitional challenges

**Persuasive Writing Prompt**

# Should regulations for food ingredients be more strict in the United States?

**Topics to consider ...**

- Consumer safety concerns
- Transparency in labeling
- Public health
- Global standards
- Increased health concerns
- Cost and affordability
- Consumer choice
- Small businesses
- Government overreach

**Persuasive Writing Prompt**

# Should movie stars make millions of dollars per movie?

**Topics to consider ...**

- Market demand
- Industry revenue
- Talent quality
- Risk and hours involved
- Income inequality
- Budget allocation
- Artistic integrity
- Alternative compensation methods

**Persuasive Writing Prompt**

# Create and argue for one new law in your hometown.

**Topics to consider ...**

- Environmental concerns
- Traffic and safety laws
- Youth engagement in the community
- Public health concerns
- Animal welfare
- Education reform
- Public spaces
- Housing and development
- Technology and privacy
- Community diversity and inclusion

**Persuasive Writing Prompt**

# Is it the responsibility of the government to provide free daycare for children?

**Topics to consider ...**

- Access to education and developmental opportunities
- Support for working families
- Social equality
- Child safety
- Economic implications
- Parental flexibility
- Public health and nutrition
- Community support and infrastructure

**Persuasive Writing Prompt**

**You've been working hard at a job for 2 years without a raise. Make a persuasive argument for your boss to give you a fair raise.**

**Topics to consider ...**

- Job performance and achievements
- Responsibilities
- Market value
- Cost of living
- Professional development
- Employee retention
- Market demand and skills
- Team collaboration
- Positive feedback
- Future goals and alignment

**Persuasive Writing Prompt**

**Persuade your parents to buy you a new car.**

**Topics to consider ...**

- Peer comparisons
- Insurance benefits
- Family needs and convenience
- Personal and academic achievements
- Resale value
- Fuel efficiency
- Independence

**Persuasive Writing Prompt**

# Is it justifiable to use animals in medical research studies?

**Topics to consider ...**

- Scientific advancements
- Alternatives
- Animal welfare standards
- Public health impact
- Ethics

**Persuasive Writing Prompt**

# Persuade your school to offer an alien language elective.

Topics to consider ...

- Artistic value
- Intellectual curiosity
- Innovation
- Student interest and engagement
- Educational morale

**Persuasive Writing Prompt**

**Write a convincing argument to your town mayor to allow citizens to plant 1,500 trees downtown.**

Topics to consider ...

- Environmental benefits
- Aesthetics
- Community engagement
- Urban green spaces
- Economic benefits
- Well-being
- Sustainability
- Educational opportunities

**Persuasive Writing Prompt**

# Should genetically modified organisms be used in agriculture?

**Topics to consider ...**

- Food security
- Nutrition
- Environmental impact
- Safety and regulations
- Consumer choice
- Farming challenges
- Ethics

**Persuasive Writing Prompt**

**Persuade your best friend to go into business selling donuts with you.**

Topics to consider ...

- Long-term growth
- Skill sets and roles
- Financial gains
- Passion and interest
- Market demand
- Unique vision

**Persuasive Writing Prompt**

# Argue whether or not dogs or cats make better pets.

**Topics to consider ...**

- Companionship and loyalty
- Independence
- Affection
- Activity
- Grooming
- Training
- Living environment
- Costs
- Lifestyle

**Persuasive Writing Prompt**

# Should a ban on single use plastics be implemented on a government level?

**Topics to consider ...**

- Industry perspective
- Public behavioral change
- Global regulations
- Economic impact
- Health concerns
- Alternatives
- Resource availability
- Waste management
- Environmental impact

**Persuasive Writing Prompt**

# Convince your caregivers to move to a new country with you.

**Topics to consider ...**

- Climate and environment
- Family support
- Finances
- Safety and security
- Social integration
- Cultural exploration
- Adventure
- Career advancement
- Educational opportunities
- Quality of life

**Persuasive Writing Prompt**

**Should the rich pay higher taxes?**

**Topics to consider ...**

- Tax loopholes and fairness
- Impact on economic growth
- Infrastructure development
- Public debt
- Social responsibility
- Economic fairness
- Government overreach
- Income equality
- Income retention

**Persuasive Writing Prompt**

# History

# Primary vs Secondary Sources

During your course of research of a historical event, you will want to stick with primary and secondary sources as much as possible. So what is the difference?

**Primary Sources**

A primary source is a source that is original to the time of the event and has not been altered. This can include journals, documents, direct quotes, recordings, emails, artifacts, diaries, manuscripts, newspaper reports, eye-witness accounts, speeches, interviews, etc. These are as close to the event as possible with the least amount of tampering. If you are thinking like a detective, these would all be the best pieces for evidence to investigate your case.

**Secondary Sources**

Secondary sources are the next step beyond a primary source, and they often reference or directly quote a primary source. Secondary sources offer interpretation of primary evidence using someone else's expertise or research. Scholarly articles, documents, critiques, biographies, or an essay could be considered secondary sources. If you are thinking like an investigator, you will rely on these less than primary sources. Secondary sources are great tools for gathering a full picture, but are more susceptible to bias or tampering than primary sources.

# Citing Sources

Citing your source, or giving credit to the source, is an important part of writing history papers. Any time you reference someone else's work, you must give them the credit so your reader can reference the larger piece of work. There is a very specific way to do this, and it can take an entire book to cover the details. There are many available books and online resources on this subject. If you are unsure how to cite sources, you can begin with a web search like, "how to cite sources for a history paper." The two major forms for citing are MLA and APA.

# Finding Reputable Sources

When referencing a source for research, it is important to establish whether or not the source is trustworthy. Here are some tips:

- Research the author. Is S/he an authority on the subject? Why do their opinions matter?
- Is the work peer reviewed?
- What type of website are you using? .com, .net, .gov, .org?
- How old is the source? Is it giving up-to-date information?
- Does the information seem unbiased?

**Finding Sources**

# Constructing a Well-Written Research Paper

**A Clear Thesis**
Just as in your persuasive writing, you will want to clearly define your thesis. You want to be specific about the point of the paper and what the reader should expect.

**Don't Skimp on Research**
You want to do a thorough job investigating your topic. A variety of quality sources will help ensure that you are getting the full picture. Using one or two sources will limit the scope of your understanding and may leave you vulnerable to writing a bias or ill-informed paper. Not only should you aim for as many primary sources as possible, but you should always try your best to verify the validity of the source. Incorporate direct quotes as much as possible as well as expert opinion, eyewitness accounts, statistics, and scholarly arguments to add depth to your analysis.

**Organization**
Are you beginning to see the common threads on what creates a well-written paper? Organization is important in writing, no matter what type of writing it may be. Research papers are no exception. Your structure should make sense, guiding the reader in a logical sequence of events to end at your conclusion. Don't forget transitional phrases to make the shift from one paragraph to the next almost seamless.

**Provide Insight**
Adding your own critical analysis makes your paper stand apart from others. Don't simply parrot what others are saying. Structure your paper in a way that supports your thesis in a unique but solid manner. Offer your analysis of the subject with plenty of supporting evidence. This is the part of writing that takes focus and creative thought as well as critical thinking. Be a detective, piecing things together. Sometimes fresh eyes see things in a light no one else has in the past, and that is where breakthroughs happen.
No one can tell a story exactly like you. Let your voice shine through in your writing.

---

**The following research prompts will require you to research a subject and write a report answering key questions or think about certain topics. Use the information you have learned about writing and citing sources to complete these writing assignments. They will take time and effort to complete - usually more than a day or two. Use the lined papers to record notes, cite sources, outline your papers, or brainstorm. When you are finished, present your paper to a parent, teacher, mentor, or friend for feedback. Don't forget, if the feedback doesn't feel positive you should not take it personally. Analyze the feedback for clues for improvement. Writing takes practice and people will not always like your opinions or points. That is okay too.**

Research Paper Tips

# The Rennaisance

Research the Rennaissance era (14th - 17th centuries) and its impact on Europe. Include the influences of the arts, intellectual developments (especially in math and science), the church, society, and politics. How do you think this period changed the course of human history?

## Things to consider as you research:

When was the Rennaissance period?

What is humanism?

What is classical learning?

What is individualism?

Did the Catholic church change during this period?

What is secularism?

What kind of exploration happened in this time period?

**The Renaissance**

Who are some of the key figures during this period?

Did any countries or regions stick out in your research?

Where did the biggest advances happen in this period?

What was trade like during this era?

What stands out most to you about this time period?

Are there any common thoughts by scholars you keep seeing about this era?

Have you found any misconceptions about this time in history?

Which important findings or inventions come from this period?

What type of music and art were most popular during this time?

**The Renaissance**

# The Atlantic Slave Trade

The Atlantic slave trade had far-reaching effects on many aspects of life across the globe. Research this era in history to write about the following:

- The origins of Atlantic slave trade and key historical events. Include key players in Europe, the African kingdoms, and people in the Americas.
- Investigate the effects on the economies in Africa, Europe, and the Americas. Include not only the effects of selling humans as commodities, but also the effects of the labor they provided to stoke the economy and global trade of goods like sugar, tobacco, rum, and cotton.
- Analyze the ethical element of all parties involved in the trade during the time. What was the general view of the time from people outside of the trade industry? Did it evolve during the years the trade was active?

How did this trade circle change the human demographics of the world?

**Things to consider as you research:**

What was the Atlantic Slave trade?

When did it start?

Which countries were involved?

Who benefited from trading these people?

What kind of African civilizations existed during this time?

Was Africa the only area from which slaves were extracted?

Who was buying African slaves?

**Atlantic Slave Trade**

Who are some of the key figures during this period?

Did any countries or regions stick out in your research?

What were some of the conflicts in Africa during this time?

What were slaves being traded for?

What stands out most to you about this time period?

Are there any ideas you keep seeing about this era?

Have you found any misconceptions about this time in history?

Did anyone express moral dilemma with buying and selling people during this period or was it completely accepted?

**Atlantic Slave Trade**

# The Napoleonic Wars

Explore the impact of the Napoleonic Wars on Europe (and France in particular). Include factors such as change in government, nationalism, military tactics, the spread of ideas, etc. Analyze the lasting impact of these wars on Europe's landscape.

# Things to consider as you research:

What were the Napoleonic Wars?

When did they happen?

Which countries were involved?

Who benefited?

What kinds of military tactics were used during this time?

How did nationalism play a role in these conflicts?

How did the wars affect the European landscape?

**Napoleonic Wars**

Who were some of the key figures during this period?

Did any countries or regions stick out in your research?

What were some of the conflicts in French society?

What did the political landscape look like?

What stands out most to you about this time period?

Are there any ideas you keep seeing about this era?

Have you found any misconceptions about this time in history?

Did the population of France support the wars? Why or why not?

**Napoleonic Wars**

# 19th Century China

Investigate major events and challenges faced by China throughout the 19th century. Choose a topic to write about. Make sure to include key names, what caused the events, all parties involved, and what the effects were, especially on the modernization of China. Topics to consider:

- The decline of the Qing Dynasty
- The Opium Wars
- Western Imperialism and Trade
- Reformation
- The Taiping Rebellion (or other internal rebellions)

**Things to consider as you research:**

What type of government existed in China during this period?

Were the citizens prospering?

Were there any major conflicts?

What kind of social climate existed during this time?

What was the state of the Chinese economy?

How did nationalism play a role in these conflicts?

What was the educational landscape at the time?

**19th Century China**

Who were some of the key figures during this period?

What kind of traditions existed in China during this period?

What did the political landscape look like?

What stands out most to you about this time period?

Have you found any misconceptions about this time in history?

What kinds of reformations were happening?

**19th Century China**

# The Fall of the Ottoman Empire

Research key factors that contributed to the eventual fall of the Ottoman Empire in the early 20th century. What caused the fall? What were the lasting effects of its collapse in the Middle East?

**Ottoman Empire**

## Things to consider as you research:

What was the Ottoman Empire?

How long did it exist?

In which area of the world did it exist?

What kinds of internal weaknesses did the empire experience before the fall?

What type of economic struggles did the empire have?

Who was the leader during the time of its collapse?

Did the empire experience any social struggles in this time?

**Ottoman Empire**

Who are some of the key figures during this period?

What kind of governance did the empire have?

What did the political landscape look like outside of the empire?

Were there any lasting effects of the fall of this empire in the Middle East?

What role did World War I play in the fall of this empire?

**Ottoman Empire**

# Australia During WWI

Australia paid a high price in casualties during the first World War, yet it is often overlooked in history books. Investigate key events in Australia's involvement in The Great War and the effects it had on the country during and after the war. How did this war affect Australia?

**Things to consider as you research:**

When did World War I begin?

Why did it begin?

Which countries were involved?

When did Australia enter the war? How did they enter?

Who controlled Australia during this time?

How many Australian troops were involved?

What were their roles in the war?

**Australia WWI**

Did you find any memorable stories in your research?

What kind of impact did Australia's involvement have on the war?

What did the political landscape look like in Australia?

Were there any lasting effects of the war in this country?

How many Australians died during the war?

What role did World War I play on Australia's sovereignty after the war?

**Australia WWI**

# The Russian Revolution and the Rise of Communism

What were the causes and effects of the Russian Revolution in the early 20th century? Analyze the key factors in overthrowing Tsar Nicholas II and the establishment of the Bolshevik party. How did this tie into the Russian Civil War? Identify key points of communist ideologies. How did this party transform within the region over time?

**Things to consider as you research:**

What was the Russian Revolution?

Why did it begin?

Who was the leader of the country at the time?

Why was there a conspiracy to overthrow them?

Why did the Bolshevik Party get established?

Who were the Red Army and the White Army?

**Russian Revolution**

Who are some of the key figures in the communist ideology at the time?

What social ideals did Karl Marx have?

How are socialism and communism related?

What kind of economic climate followed the revolution?

Were there any lasting effects of the war in this country?

How many Russians died during the Revolution and the Civil War?

**Russian Revolution**

# The Manhattan Project

Research the origins, development, and effects of the Manhattan Project. How was this project tied to dropping the atomic bomb on Hiroshima and Nagasaki? What were the effects of the creation of the bomb by the Americans on the outcome of the second World War?

**Things to consider as you research:**

What was the Manhattan Project?

Why did it begin?

Who were some of the major players in the project?

What was the mission of the project?

Which countries were involved?

What challenges did the scientists face?

What were the scientific motivations for the project?

**The Manhattan Project**

Were the political motivations more compelling or less compelling than the scientific motivations?

Did you find any memorable stories in your research?

Where are Hiroshima and Nagasaki?

Why were these the locations chosen for dropping bombs during WWII?

What were the long-term effects of the bombs being dropped in Japan?

How many Japanese citizens were affected?

Did any of the scientists who were part of this project ever publicly express regret in being part of it?

**The Manhattan Project**

# The Korean War

What were major events during the war and how did the war affect the dynamics of the Cold war? Include key factors such as the split of North and South Korea, the tensions between communist and capitalist ideologies, the role of the U.S., the Soviet Union, and China, and military tactics. What do you think came out of this war?

_____
_____
_____
_____
_____
_____
_____
_____
_____
_____
_____
_____
_____
_____
_____
_____
_____
_____
_____
_____
_____

**Things to consider as you research:**

What was the Korean War?

Who was involved?

Why are there two Korean countries?

When did the countries split?

What is the historical context leading up to the war?

Who were relevant political leaders?

**The Korean War**

How did capitalism play a role i n this conflict?

How did communism play a role?

What were the ties to the Cold War?

What is the 38th parallel? Why is it a DMZ?

What was the result of this war?

**The Korean War**

# The Berlin Wall

Describe the history of the Berlin Wall from construction to demolition. What was the significance of the wall figuratively and literally? Pay particular attention to policies and political decisions.

**Things to consider as you research:**

What was the Berlin wall?

Where was it?

Who built it?

When was it built?

What was its purpose?

What did it represent?

**The Berlin Wall**

What did it separate?

How did citizens of both sides feel about the wall?

What were the ties to the Cold War?

Who were relevant leaders during the time of its existence and what were their political roles?

When was it removed?

Why was it removed?

What did this symbolize?

**The Berlin Wall**

# The Space Race

Explain the space race between the United States and the USSR during the Cold War. Include key factors in the origins of the space race, important figures, political rivalries that caused the conflict, and milestones and achievements in the race. Did the public support these efforts? What were the lasting effects of this conflict on the world?

**Things to consider as you research:**

What was the space race?

Who were key figures involved?

Which countries were involved?

When did it begin?

Why did it begin?

What was the goal? Why?

**The Space Race**

What did this have to do with the Cold War?

How was this tied to the war on communism?

What were some of the important milestones in the race?

What came out of the space race?

How did it change history?

Was there a winner?

**The Space Race**

# The Apartheid of South Africa

Explain the origins of the apartheid. Make sure to include key topics such as colonialism, racial segregation, and racial classification. What events led to the end of the apartheid? How has the region recovered from its effects? How do we prevent events like this in the future?

**Apartheid**

**Things to consider as you research:**

What does apartheid mean?

Who were key figures involved?

Which groups of people were involved?

When did it begin?

Why did it begin?

What were some specific policies and laws that enabled the apartheid? Who passed them? Why?

**Apartheid**

What was happening in this area before it was enacted?

What effect did this have on citizens?

Has this ever happened in other areas of the world?

How was colonialism connected to this?

How did it change history?

How did it end? Does the area have any lasting effects?

**Apartheid**

# Security After 9/11

Analyze the effects of the terrorist attack in NYC on September 11, 2001 on global security. How did governments respond? What were some of the counter terrorism policies adopted in the aftermath of the attack? What price have civilians and military service members paid in the name of security? How do we balance personal privacy and security?

**Things to consider as you research:**

What happened on September 11, 2001 in New York City?

Who were key figures involved?

Which groups of people were involved? Which countries?

What was the significance of the two buildings that were struck?

Were any other buildings struck?

What were the historical circumstances between the United States and al-Qaeda leading up to this attack?

Post 9/11

How many people were lost in the attack?

What was the response of the United States government to the attack?

What US agencies were formed as a direct result of this day?

What significant policies came as a result of this attack?

How did the way the world deals with national security change?

How has personal privacy been affected as a result of this attack?

**Post 9/11**

# Current Events

Look to headlines for current world events. Dive deeper. How do these events tie in with historical events, politics, and government policies of the countries involved? Can you see any parallels between this current event and other historical events in other parts of the world? Are there any common themes?

**Things to consider as you research:**

What is this event?

Who were key figures involved?

Which groups of people were involved? Which countries?

What is the significance of this event?

How is it tied to past events?

**Current Events**

What are the future implications?

Can you find any past policies which have contributed to this event?

Can you think of any future policies which may result?

How does this affect you?

# Science

# Plant cell

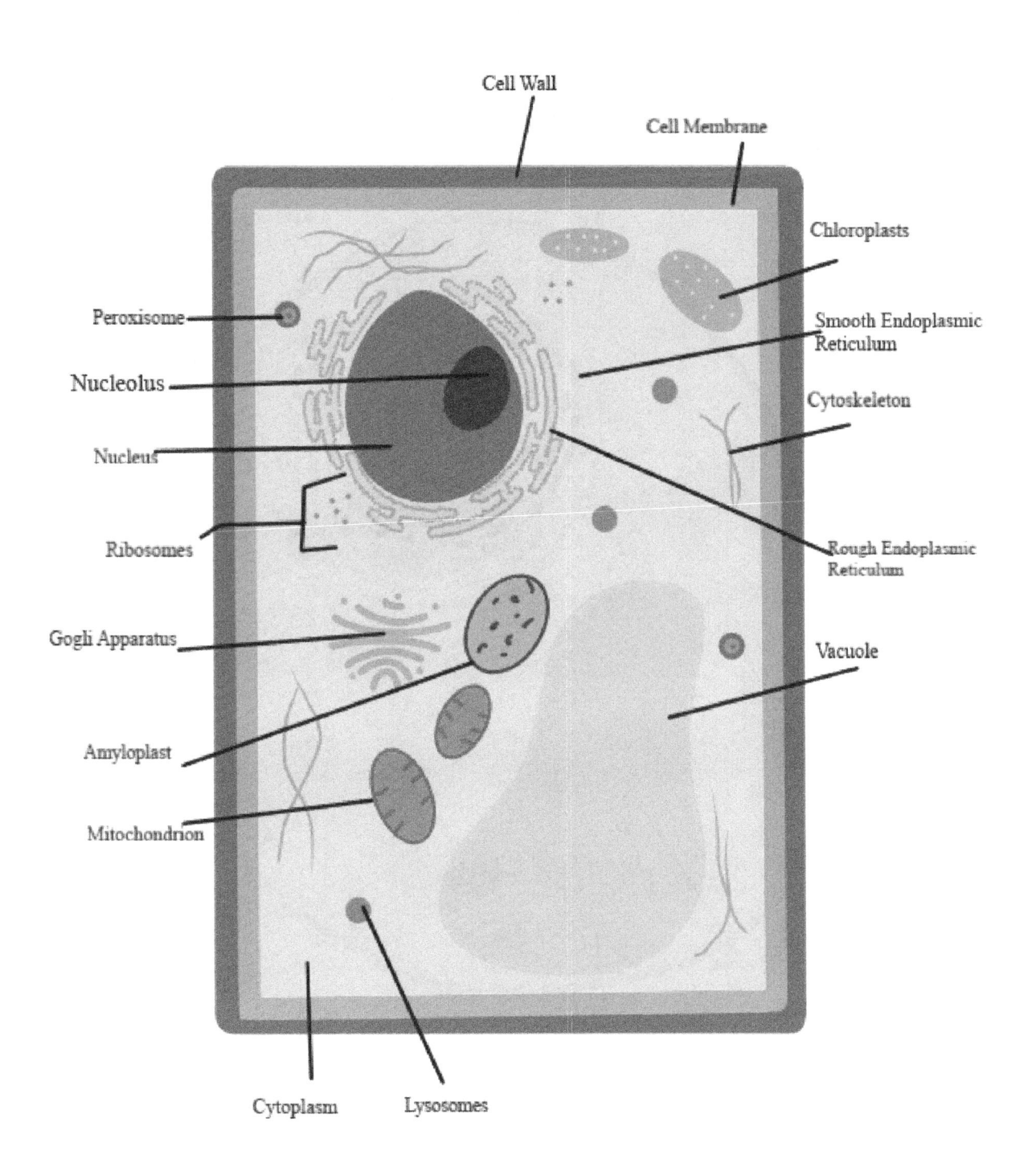

Cell Wall
Cell Membrane
Chloroplasts
Peroxisome
Smooth Endoplasmic Reticulum
Nucleolus
Cytoskeleton
Nucleus
Rough Endoplasmic Reticulum
Ribosomes
Gogli Apparatus
Vacuole
Amyloplast
Mitochondrion
Cytoplasm
Lysosomes

Cells

# Animal Cell

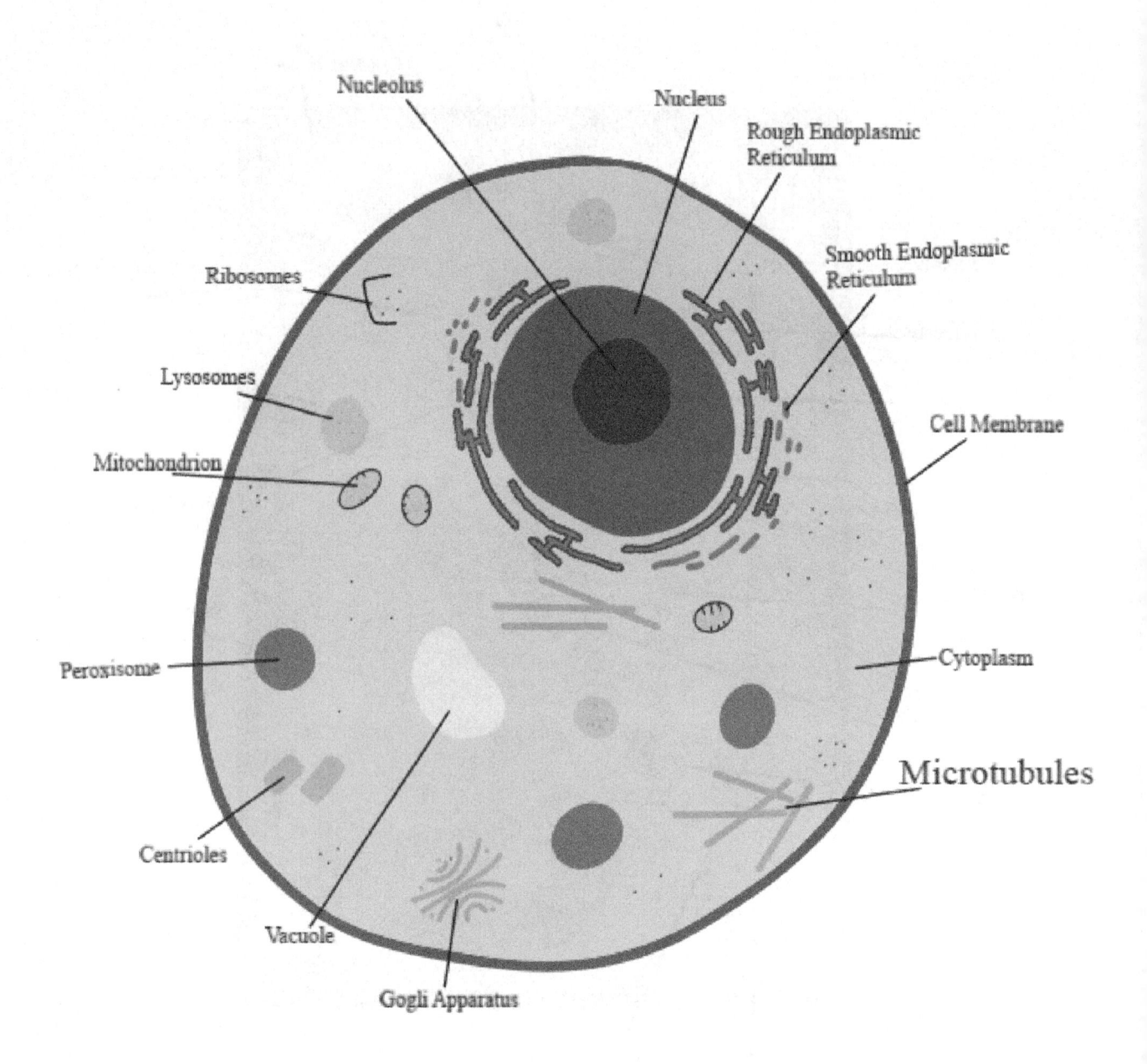

- Nucleolus
- Nucleus
- Rough Endoplasmic Reticulum
- Ribosomes
- Smooth Endoplasmic Reticulum
- Lysosomes
- Mitochondrion
- Cell Membrane
- Peroxisome
- Cytoplasm
- Microtubules
- Centrioles
- Vacuole
- Gogli Apparatus

Cells

# Mitosis

Parent Cell

Prophase

Metaphase

Anaphase

Telophase

Cells

# Biology Study Questions

1. What is the function of a cell membrane?

It is an outer boundary of a cell, and is semipermeable. That means it lets things pass into the cell selectively. It's also flexible, so it lets the cell move in many different ways.

2. What does a plant need to perform photosynthesis? What are the products of this process?

It needs algae and some bacteria to produce glucose using light, water, and carbon dioxide.

3. Explain cellular respiration.

Cellular respiration happens after glucose is available, and is the process of that glucose being turned into ATP, which is a molecule that cells extract energy from.

**Biology Questions**

# Biology Study Questions

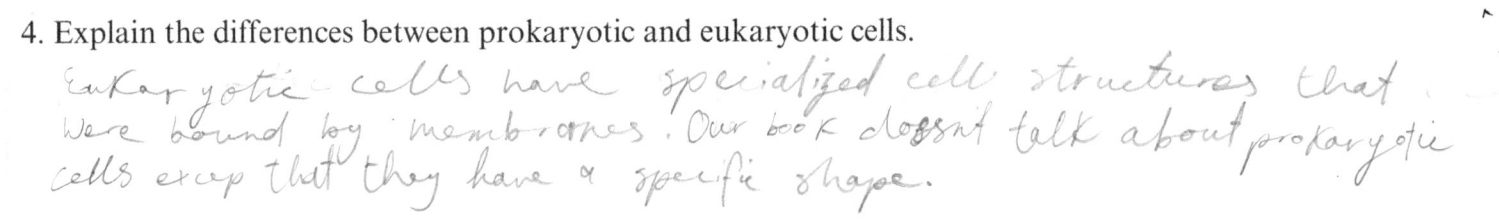

4. Explain the differences between prokaryotic and eukaryotic cells.

Eukaryotic cells have specialized cell structures that were bound by membranes. Our book doesn't talk about prokaryotic cells except that they have a specific shape.

5. What is the difference between mitosis and meiosis?

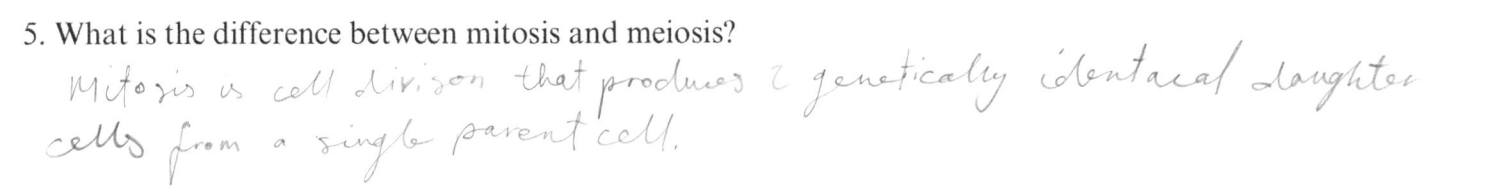

Mitosis is cell division that produces 2 genetically identical daughter cells from a single parent cell.

6. What is the significance of mitosis in the repair of injured or damaged tissue?

7. What are some key differences between animal and plant cells?

**Biology Questions**

# Biology Study Questions

8. Explain the function of DNA and its structure.

9. What is the difference between a dominant and a recessive gene?

10. How do DNA and RNA differ?

11. Explain the concept of symbiosis.

# Biology Study Questions

12. What do animal cells need to survive?

13. What is an enzyme?

14. What is a macromolecule? Give some examples. What are their functions?

15. What is a polymer?

Biology Questions

# Biology Study Questions

16. Describe the difference between covalent and ionic bonds.

17. What is an ion?

18. What is the role of electrolytes in the body?

**Biology Questions**

# Effects of pH on Enzyme Activity

## Abstract:
Enzymes are naturally produced catalysts for biochemical reactions in living things. Enzymes can be affected by the pH of their environment. In this experiment, we will investigate how pH affects the enzyme catalase. Catalase is the enzyme responsible for the breakdown of hydrogen peroxide ($H_2O_2$) into oxygen ($O_2$) and water ($H_2O$).

## Objective:
To observe the effects of various pH environments on the rate of activity of the enzyme catalase by measuring the height of the bubbles resulting from the enzyme breaking down the $H_2O_2$ into $O_2$ and $H_2O$.

## Materials:
- Dry active yeast
- 3% hydrogen peroxide solution
- Solutions of varying pH levels (acidic, neutral, and alkaline i.e vinegar, milk, baking soda in water, etc.)
- pH test strips
- Test tubes and test tube rack
- Graduated cylinder
- Stopwatch
- Ruler
- 1/2 teaspoon
- Safety goggles
- Lab Coat
- Gloves
- A parent (adult supervision)

## Precautions:
Always wear protective equipment when performing science labs. This includes eye protection, gloves, and protective cloth over your skin. Always take caution when mixing any chemicals. First research the chemical reactions they may have together as they could produce harmful fumes and cause health effects when breathed. Research the buffer solutions you will be using in this experiment. Never mix substances without researching first. When in doubt, ask a trusted adult for help.

Continued.

**Biology Lab**

# Effects of pH on Enzyme Activity Continued

**Procedure:**

1. Equip personal protective equipment.
2. Add an equal amount of hydrogen peroxide solution to each test tube.
3. Prepare buffer solutions (milk, distilled water, saliva, vinegar, etc.) and add an equal amount of a different solution in each tube.
4. Use the pH test strips to test the pH of each tube and label it accordingly.
5. Start the stopwatch.
6. Add 1/2 teaspoon yeast to each test tube and quickly add a stopper to the top.
7. Measure the height of the bubbles formed every 45 seconds for a period of 3 minutes.
8. Analyze your data.

**Analysis:**

Calculate the enzyme activity by analyzing the height of the bubbles in each solution at various time intervals and graph the changes of enzyme activity according to the pH of its environment. Analyze the results and identify the patterns. What are your findings? Was your hypothesis correct? Which pH was best for enzyme activity? What are your conclusions about this experiment? What could have been changed to make the experiment better?

**Biology Lab**

# Data Log

**Experiment Title:**

**Objective:**

**Hypothesis:**

**Procedure:**

**Observations/ Results:**

**Conclusion:**

**Biology Lab**

# Effects of Temperature on Seed Germination

## Objectives:
To explore the effects of temperature on the germination of seeds of varying plant species by placing the planted seeds in different temperatures.

## Materials:
- Seed starting pots
- Seeds of at least 3 plant species (Hint: choose seeds that have a similar, quick germination time like beans, lentils, chives, radishes)
- Potting soil (or damp paper towels on a plate if you do not have pots and soil)
- Water
- Marker
- Heating and cooling sources and thermometer
- Ruler
- Data log
- Personal protection equipment (goggles, gloves, lab coat, etc.)

## Precautions:
Always wear protective equipment when performing science labs. This includes eye protection, gloves, and protective cloth over your skin. When using heating or cooling sources, take care in keeping anything flammable away from the heating source. Be sure not to heat it too hot as to avoid fire. Also take care in cold to protect the skin from exposure. Your temperatures should not reach such extremes for this experiment. When in doubt, ask a trusted adult for help.

## Procedure:
1. Equip personal protection equipment.
2. Label each pot with the type of seed that will be placed into it. You will want one pot per seed type in each temperature location. It is recommended to use more than one seed per pot. For example, three sweet pea seeds in a pot. If you are using the countertop, the fridge, and your back porch as locations, you will need pots with each seed in each location.
3. Fill each pot with equal amount of soil and water with equal amount of water to dampen the soil.
4. Plant seeds according to the recommended depths. If you are using paper towels, dampen them and fold in half before placing the seed, then fold in half again and place on the labeled plate or dish.
5. Place the prepared seeds in their various environments. Environments with controlled temperatures work best (like a refrigerator) but if you don't have these, use an area that stays generally the same temperature.
6. Monitor germination daily for the emergence of seedlings. Keep soil or paper towels moist. Be sure to record what you observe in equal increments of time on your log even if you don't observe any change. Measure growth, record the temperature, number of sprouts, amount of time until germination, etc. for two weeks.

## Analysis:
Calculate the germination period for each seed in each location. Graph the results. Analyze patterns and data. What do you see? What are your conclusions about this experiment? Was your hypothesis correct? What could have been done differently to give more accurate results?

**Biology Lab**

# Data Log

**Biology Lab**

**Experiment Title:**

**Objective:**

**Hypothesis:**

**Procedure:**

**Observations/ Results:**

**Conclusion:**

**Biology Lab**

# Effects of Light Color on Plant Growth

## Objectives:
To explore the effects of light color on the rate of growth in plants by placing seeds under colored plastic.

## Materials:
- 3 or more 2 Liter plastic bottles
- The same number of pots with water trays (make sure they will be able to fit under the bottom half of the soda bottle)
- Seeds of 1 plant type (Hint: choose seeds that have quick germination time like beans, lentils, chives, or radishes)
- Potting soil
- Water
- Colored permanent markers if you cannot find three different colored plastic bottles
- Ruler
- Data log
- Scissors
- PPE

## Precautions:
Always wear protective equipment when performing science labs. This includes eye protection, gloves, and protective cloth over your skin. Be sure to protect your hands when cutting and coloring the plastic. If using markers, be sure to stay in a well-ventilated area. When in doubt, ask a trusted adult for help.

## Procedure:
1. Equip personal protection equipment.
2. Label each pot with the color light it will be placed beneath.
3. Fill each pot with equal amounts of soil.
4. Plant seeds according to the recommended depths. Place the same number of seeds per pot.
5. Place the pots on the water trays with equal amounts of water in each tray.
6. Carefully cut the plastic bottles in half. Discard or use the top half for another purpose. If your bottles are all clear, choose three colors and color the bottles. Be sure each is a different color.
7. Place the pots in a sunny location and place the coordinating bottle bottom upside down over each pot.
8. Observe plant germination and growth over a two-week period. Record observations in equal intervals such as every day. Try recording observations at the same time each day. Record growth, color changes, appearance of vitality or sickness, how many seeds sprout, etc. Be sure to keep the plants under the light filters except when they need watered.

## Analysis:
Analyze the data. Chart or graph growth for each light filter. Identify patterns. What are your findings? What is your conclusion based on this experiment? Was your hypothesis correct? What could have been done differently to make the experiment better?

**Biology Lab**

# Data Log

**Experiment Title:**

**Objective:**

**Hypothesis:**

**Procedure:**

**Observations/ Results:**

**Conclusion:**

**Biology Lab**

# The Effects of Sodium Bicarbonate on Photosynthesis

## Objectives:
To observe the effects of adding sodium bicarbonate (baking soda) to a solution containing leaf disks by measuring the time it takes for half the disks to float. The floating disks will be caused by oxygen production during photosynthesis.

## Materials:
- Spinach leaves
- Single hole punch
- Light source
- Syringe (at least 10 mL)
- Baking Soda (Sodium bicarbonate) to act as the carbon dioxide source
- Water
- 1/4 teaspoon
- Measuring cup
- 2 clear cups
- Paper towels
- PPE
- Dish soap

## Precautions:
Always wear protective equipment when performing science labs. This includes eye protection, gloves, and protective cloth over your skin. When in doubt, ask a trusted adult for help.

## Procedure:
1. Equip personal protection equipment.
2. Label one clear cup "water" and the other "NaHCO3" (sodium bicarbonate)
3. To the cup labeled NaHCO3 add 250 mL water, 1/4 teaspoon sodium bicarbonate, and one drop dish soap. (The dish soap allows the water to wet the surface of the leaf.) To the other cup add the water and soap only. Mix the NaHCO3 solution carefully to avoid making any suds until the solution is completely dissolved. Carefully stir the water and soap solution as well.
4. Set up your light source if you do not have a place with direct sunlight.
5. Punch out 20 circles from the spinach leaves.
6. Place 10 leaf disks inside the syringe. Carefully push the plunger until it is almost the whole way down, leaving a little space for the leaf disks so they do not get smashed. Place the syringe into the water cup and suck up some water. Push out as much air as possible. Place a finger over the opening of the syringe and pull the plunger a few times to create a vacuum. Hold the vacuum and swirl the disks. Continue doing this until all the disks sink.
7. Remove the plunger and pour the solution and leaf disks back into the cup.
8. Repeat steps 6 and 7 for the sodium bicarbonate solution cup.

Continued on the next page.

**Biology Lab**

## Procedure:

8. Place both cups beneath your light source so they receive full light.
9. Start the timer.
10. Write down your initial observations. What do you see?
11. Record observation every minute including how many disks are floating. Gently swirl solutions periodically so disks do not stick to cups.
13. Continue steps 10-12 until half the disks float.
14. You can restart this experiment and change the variables such as light intensity, sodium bicarbonate concentration, temperature, leaf types, etc.
15. Record and analyze your data.

## Analysis:

Analyze the data. Chart or graph the number of floating disks by minutes for each cup. Identify patterns. What are your findings? What is your conclusion based on this experiment? Was your hypothesis correct? What could have been done differently to make the experiment better? What is the median time for floating in each cup? How do they compare?

**Biology Lab**

# Data Log

**Experiment Title:**

**Objective:**

**Hypothesis:**

**Procedure:**

**Observations/ Results:**

**Conclusion:**

**Biology Lab**

# Explore Nutrient Absorption by Plants with Colored Water

## Objectives:
To investigate nutrient absorption by plants by placing cut flowers in colored water to see the absorption and transport of the colored water.

## Materials:
- Cut white flowers with long stems (carnations work well)
- Pack of multi colored food dye
- Clear containers such as vases, glasses, or canning jars
- Water
- Spoon for stirring
- PPE

## Precautions:
Always wear protective equipment when performing science labs. This includes eye protection, gloves, and protective cloth over your skin. When in doubt, ask a trusted adult for help.

## Procedure:
1. Equip personal protection equipment.
2. Fill each container 3/4 full with water.
3. Add one color dye to each container, making each container of water a different color. Make sure they are saturated with enough dye to make a deep color. Stir.
4. Make a 45° angle cut at the end of each flower stem to allow for more surface area on the cut.
5. Place one flower in each container.
6. Record your observations of each container. Flower color, stem color, leaf color, flower health, water level, etc.
7. Record observations after 2 hours and then again after 8 hours (or overnight).
8. Analyze findings.

## Analysis:
Analyze your data. Did the flowers, stems, or leaves change color? Were any colors more noticeable in the plant than others? Could you replicate this with other types of white flowers? How does this relate to the way plants absorb nutrients and water from their roots? What could you have done differently in this experiment? What can you conclude from this experiment? Was your hypothesis correct?

**Biology Lab**

# Data Log

**Experiment Title:**

**Objective:**

**Hypothesis:**

**Procedure:**

**Observations/ Results:**

**Conclusion:**

**Biology Lab**

# Finding Traits in Offspring Using the Punnet Square

**Abstract:**

A Punnet Square is a tool named after British scientist Reginald Punnet used to predict the possible genotypes and phenotypes of offspring based on the genotype of the parents. We will be using a simple Punnett square in this experiment, focusing on single genes with two alleles from each parent. Many traits or phenotypes arise from multiple genes (such as eye color), but for the sake of this experiment we will assume the phenotypes arise from one gene.

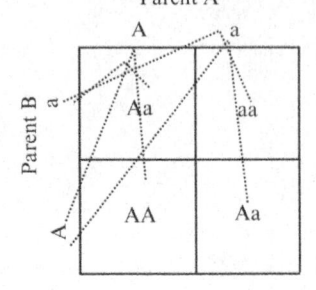

In this example, both parents have an Aa allele combination. Setting the Punnett Square up to show Parent A's alleles across the top of the Square grid and Parent B along the side, we can find the intersection of the alleles to see the offsprings' genotype possibilities. If A represents a dominant gene and a represents a recessive, we can see that the probability of the offspring showing a recessive phenotype is 1/4.

## Objectives:

To explore phenotype possibilities by examining random genotype combinations using a simple Punnett Square model.

## Precautions:

Always wear protective equipment when performing science labs. This includes eye protection, gloves, and protective cloth over your skin. When in doubt, ask a trusted adult for help.

## Materials:

- Punnett Square worksheet provided
- Colored objects such as beans or beads. Be sure there are only two colors and they are all the same size and shape. Have 4 of each.
- A bag, hat, box, or other container you cannot see through.
- PPE

Continued.

**Biology Lab**

# Finding Traits in Offspring Using the Punnet Square

## Procedure:

1. Equip personal protection equipment.
2. Place all colored objects in your container.
3. Decide which color will represent the dominant trait and which will represent a recessive trait. Example: the red bead represents a dominant trait like a red flower, and the blue represents the recessive like a white flower. Write this key down beside your Punnett Square.
4. Pull two objects from the container without looking. These will be the alleles for Parent A. Write the alleles in the Punnett Square places for Parent A.
5. Repeat step 4 for Parent B.
6. Use the graph to find the allele combinations for the offspring.
7. Repeat this for the other Squares. If you would like to keep going, make more squares.
8. Determine the genotypes and phenotypes of each offspring. Analyze your results.

## Analysis:

Analyze your data. Identify patterns. What are the ratios of genotypes and phenotypes observed? Were these results expected? How did the results compare to your hypothesis? What kind of environmental factors could change the results? What are your conclusions from performing the experiment?

**Biology Lab**

# Punnett Square Worksheet

**Biology Lab**

**Experiment Title:**

**Objective:**

**Hypothesis:**

**Procedure:**

**Observations/ Results:**

**Conclusion:**

**Biology Lab**

# Solutions

# Math

## Page 3

Solution 1:

Using $a^2+b^2=c^2$.   $c^2=4^2+3^2$   $c^2=16+9$   $c^2=25$   $c=5$ feet

Solution 2:

Let the angles be 1x, 2x, and 3x. Solve for x

1x+2x+3x=180.   x=30.   1x=30°   2x= 60°   3x=90°

Solution 3:

Let's call the missing length x.   $8^2+x^2=17^2$   $64+x^2=289$   $x^2= 289-64$   $x^2=225$   $x=\sqrt{225}$   x=15   15m

## Page 4

Solution 4:

$\cos(45°)= 1/(\sqrt{2})$   $\cos(45°)= \frac{\text{Adjacent}}{\text{hypotenuse}} = 12/x$   $x=12/\cos(45°) \approx 16.97$ feet

Solution 5:

A right triangle must follow the $a^2+b^2=c^2$ rule, with $c^2$ being the greatest value. So, $AB^2+AC^2= BC^2$   $8^2+6^2=10^2$   $64+36=100$   Yes, this satisfies the Pythagorean Theorem and is a right triangle.

Solution 6:

All triangles have 3 angles equalling 180°. Since these angles fulfill this criteria, we must now decide the type of triangle. Since all angles are less than 90° the triangle is acute.

Solution 7:

The tower, it's shadow, and the ground form a right triangle, so we will use tan(55°). Let the height of the tower be h.

Tan(55°)= opposite/adjacent = h/4   h= 4 × tan(55°) ≈ 5.712 yards.   5.71 yards

# Math

## Page 5

Solution 8:
The sum of all exterior angles on a regular polygon will equal 360°. If we take the total sum of the angles divided by the measure of each angle, we get the number of sides (n). Therefore, 360°/30° = 12.  n=12 sides

Solution 9:
360°/90°= 4. n=4 sides

Solution 10:
Area of a rectangle = Length × Width  The area needed for the goat pen is
15 ft² × 2 goats = 30 ft². Next we find all the factors of 30 to see the possible dimensions, which include:  5'×6', 6'×5', 10'×3', 3'×10', 2'×15', 15'×2'

Solution 11:
Perimeter of a rectangle = 2 × (length + width)
2 × (6+5)   2 × (11) = 22ft  You should buy at least 22 feet of fencing.

## Page 6

Solution 12:
First, let's get all terms into the same unit of measure, inches.
Length = 60 inches
width = 48 inches
height = 2 inches    Volume = L × W × H  = 5,760 in.
cubic foot in inches = 12 × 12 × 12 = 1,728   Convert volume to cubic ft.  5760/1728 = 3.333ft³
Since each bag only covers 2 ft³, you will need to buy 2 bags.

Solution 13:
Area of a trapezoid: ½ (a+b) × h    a and b are the lengths of the parallel sides and h is the height between them. ½ (3 + 5.5) × 3   ½ (8.5) × 3   4.25 × 3   A = 12.75 m

# Math

## Page 6
**Solution 14:**
Perimeter = length/side × n sides. Since a pentagon has 5 sides, n=5
8cm × 5 = 40 cm

## Page 7
**Solution 15:**
Use the quadratic formula from page 2 and plug in the values a=1, b=4, and c=5.

$$x = \frac{-4 \pm \sqrt{4^2 - 4(1)(5)}}{2 \cdot 1} \quad \frac{-4 \pm \sqrt{4-20}}{2} \quad \frac{-4 \pm \sqrt{-4}}{2}$$

because ($b^2-4ac$) is negative, the solutions will be complex numbers so x=

$$\frac{-4 \pm 2i}{2}. \quad x = -4/2 \pm 2i/2 \quad x = -2 \pm i \quad x = -2 + i \text{ and } x = -2 - i$$

**Solution 16:**

$x^2+2x+2=4 \quad x^2+2x-2=0 \quad a=1 \; b=2 \; c=-2 \quad x = \frac{-2 \pm \sqrt{2^2 - 4(1)(-2)}}{2(1)} \quad x = \frac{-2 \pm \sqrt{4+8}}{2}$

$x = \frac{-2 \pm \sqrt{12}}{2} \quad x = \frac{-2 \pm 2\sqrt{3}}{2} \quad x = -1 + \sqrt{3} \text{ and } x = -1 - \sqrt{3}$

**Solution 17:**
We can factor to make (x-2)(x-3)=0. Using the zero product property of factors we can set each factor equal to 0 and find the value of x.   x-2=0  x-3=0  x=2 and x=3

**Solution 18:**
First move your constant to make $x^2+6x=3$. Take ½ the coefficient of x and square it. Then add and subtract it.  $x^2 + 6x + (3)^2 - (3)^2 = 3$.   $x^2 + 6x + 9 - 9 = 3$   $(x + 3)^2 - 9 = 3$   $(x + 3)^2 = 12$
$x+3=\pm\sqrt{12}$   $x+3=\pm\sqrt{4 \times 3}$   $x+3=\pm 2\sqrt{3}$   $x=-3\pm 2\sqrt{3}$   $x=-3+2\sqrt{3}$ and $x=-3-2\sqrt{3}$

## Page 8
**Solution 19:**
Solve the first equation for y.   y = 5 - x.   Substitute the value of y into the second equation.
2x - (5 - x) =7 Solve for x.   2x - 5 + x = 7   3x - 5 = 7   3x = 12   x = 4
x + y = 5   4 + y = 5   y = 1   Answer: (4,1)

# Math

**Page 8**

Solution 20:

$x = 7 - y$   $(7-y) - y = 3$   $7 - 2y = 3$   $-2y = -7 - 3$   $-2y = -4$   $y = 2$.
Now substitute the value of y into an original equation to find x.   $x + (2) = 7$
$x = 5$   Answer: (5, 2)

Solution 21:

Solve for y in terms of x.   $y = 10 - 2x$   $x - 3(10 - 2x) = 5$   $x - 30 + 6x = 5$
$7x - 30 = 5$   $7x = 35$   $x = 5$. Substitute the value of x in one of the original equations.   $2(5) + y = 10$   $10 + y = 10$   $y = 0$   Answer: (5,0)

**Page 9**

Solution 22:

First, we can eliminate the y terms. $(2x + 3y) + (x - 3y) = 15 + 3$
$3x = 18$   $x = 6$   Now we can plug the value of x into one of the original equations to find the value of y as in: $(6) - 3y = 3$   $-3y = -3$   $y = -3/-3$   $y = 1$
Answer: (6,1)

Solution 23:

Let's eliminate x. $(x + 2y = 5)(-2)$   $2x + 3y = 6 - 2x - 4y = -10$   $-y = -4$   $y = 4$
$2x + 3(4) = 6$   $2x + 12 = 6$   $2x = -6$   $x = -3$   Answer: (-3,4)

Solution 24:

First, we can eliminate the y terms by adding the equations:

   $2x + 3y = 8$                          $2(1) + 3y = 8$
$+ \; 4x - 3y = -2.$                 $2 + 3y = 8$
   $6x \;\;\;\;\; = 6$   $x = 6/6$   $x = 1$        $3y = 8 - 2$
                                        $3y = 6$   $y = 6/3$   $y = 2$

Answer: (1,2)

# Math

## Page 10

Solution 25:
$3x - 5 \geq 10$   $3x \geq 15$   $x \geq 5$

Solution 26:
$6x + 12 < 4x - 10$   $2x < -22$   $x < -11$

Solution 27:

Solution 28:
Because there is a filled circle above the 5 with the filled line extending right, this will be included in the solution set along with values greater than 5. Because the circle above 12 is open, it will be less than but not including values of 12.  $5 \leq x < 12$

## Page 11

Solution 29:
Using slipe-intercept form $y = mx + b$, we can see the slope, m, is 3 and the y intercept, b, is 5.

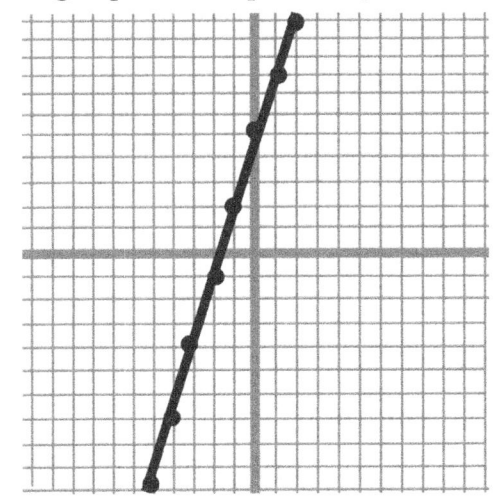

# Math

**Page 11**

Solution 30:
First we will find the slope with the formula $m = \frac{y_2 - y_1}{x_2 - x_1}$   $m = \frac{6 - 0}{0 - 3}$
$m = 6/-3$   $m = -2$   To find the y intercept (b) we can take our slope intercept formula $y = mx + b$ and isolate b to make $b = y - mx$. We will use this new formula and plug in our coordinates (3,0) or (x,y) and our slope (-2).   $b = (0) - ((-2) \times 3)$   $b = 6$   (We could have also figured this out by looking at the second coordinate, (0, 6) and understanding that it passes through the y axis at that point, therefore is the y intercept.)
Now enter all values into the slope-intercept form and get $y = -2x + 6$

**Page 12**

Solution 31:
To find the x-coordinate of the vertex, $x = \frac{-b}{2a}$   $a = 1$   $b = 4$   $c = -5$
$x = \frac{-(4)}{2(1)}$   $x = -2$   To find the y-coordinate we plug the value of x into the function. $f(-2) = (-2)^2 + 4(-2) - 5$   $y = 4-8-5$   $y = -9$
So, the vertex is located at the coordinates (-2,-9), which means the axis of symmetry is $x = -2$, and since the value of a in the equation is positive, the parabola opens upward.

Solution 32:
$a = -1$   $b = 2$   $x = -\frac{(2)}{2(-1)}$   $x = 1$   $f(1) = -(1)^2 + 2(1) + 3$   $f(1) = 4$   $y = 4$
so the vertex is at the point (1, 4).
Since the value of a is negative, our parabola opens downward and our line of symmetry is at the x value of the vertex, $x = 1$

Solution 33:
No. A quadratic function is an equation that is graphically represented by a symmetric curve that opens upward or downward with a line of symmetry through the vertical axis.

# Math

**Page 13**

Solution 34:
We can use the formula for exponential growth to solve this since our rate of growth is constant. We can use viewers (v) and time (t) to solve $v(t) = V_0 \times 2^{\frac{t}{8}}$
$V(t)$ = # of views at time (t)   $V_0$ = Initial views   t = time in hours. We use 2 because the views are doubling. Now let's plug in our known values
$1,000,000 = 200 \times 2^{\frac{t}{8}}$   $1,000,000/200 = (200 \times 2(t/8))/200$
$5,000 = 2^{\frac{t}{8}}$   $\log_2(5,000) = \frac{t}{8}$   $t = 8 \times \log_2(5,000)$   $\log_2(5,000) \approx 12.2877$
$t = 8 \times 12.2877$   $t = 98.30$ hours

Solution 35:
First, we see we have a logarithmic base of 2, so we will use that base to find the value of x. Because our logarithmic base 2 (x) is equal to 3, we will raise the base, 2, to the third power and find the value of x.   $2^3 = 8$   $x = 8$

Solutuin 36:
A logarithm tells you how many times the base must be multiplied to get to the desired output. For example, if I have a $\log_{10}(1,000) = x$ tells me my base (10) will be raised x amount of times to arrive at the argument 1,000. So we are asking to what power is 10 raised to reach 1,000? $10^3 = 1000$ so $x = 3$. If we had $\log_{10}(y) = 3$ we would see our base (10) needs raised to the power of 3 to get the argument 1,000.
Logarithms help simplify calculations, especially as you reach more complex mathematics with large numbers. They can be used to find things like exponential growth, decay, and compounding interest.

# Page 14

Solution 37:
w = width   L = w/2   perimeter = 2 ( L + w )   16 = 2 ( (w/2) + w)
16 = 2 ((w/2) + (2w/2))   16 = 2 (3w/2) the 2's cancel out giving 16 = 3w   w = 16/3
w = 5.33 cm   16 = 2 ( L + 5.33)   16 = 2L + 10.66   5.34 = 2L   L = 2.67 cm

# Math

**Page 14**

Solution 38:
Distance = Speed × time   so   distance = 65 × 3.5   distance = 227.5 km

Solution 39:
time = $\frac{\text{distance}}{\text{speed}}$   $\frac{465}{55}$   time ≈ 8.45 hours   4:00 - ( 8 hr 45 min + 1 hr) = 6:15 am

you must leave no later than 6:15 am to make it by 4 pm

**Page 15**

Solution 40:

Speed = $\frac{\text{distance}}{\text{Time}}$   first convert min to hr   $\frac{48 \text{ min}}{60 \text{ min}}$   0.8 hr

$\frac{55 \text{ km}}{0.8 \text{ hr}}$ ≈ 68.75 km/h

Solution 41:
First, find total income/ week. 13×17 = $221/week. Next find the total time it will take in weeks, to save for the total of the phone.
850/ 221 ≈ 3.85 weeks. Since he can't collect partial paychecks, it will take Allen 4 weeks of working and saving.

Solution 42:
First, we will convert all units of measure to the same as our tiles, inches. So, 8 feet × 12 in/ ft = 96 inches. 6 feet × 12 in/ft = 72 inches. Next, we will find the total area of the bathroom floor: 96 × 72 = 6,912 in². If each tile is 6 in × 6 in, the area of each tile is 36 in². So, 6,912/36 = 192 tiles.

# Math

**Page 16**

Solution 43:
$\frac{2}{3} = \frac{x}{5}$   cross multiply  $3x = 10$   $x = 10/3$   $x = 3.33$ m

Solution 44:
First let's figure out the prices after the discounts, and then we will compare the two. Store A: $700 × .15 = $105 discount. $700 - $105 = $595
Store B: $650 × .10 = $65 discount. $650 - $65 = $585. Store B has a better deal.

Solution 45:
First, find the total cost. $866 + ($115 × 7) = $1671     $1671/7 = $238.71

# History

## Important notes on the Rennaissance

The Rennaissance means "rebirth." This period is known as a time of intellectual and artistic revival in Europe from around the 14th century - 17th century. It was a transitioning period between the middle ages to the early modern age. This transition took a sharp turn from focus on religion to focus on more secular topics in music and art. With this, art changed from more symbolic to realism. Notable names during this period are Leonardo da Vinci, Michelangelo, Botticelli, William Shakespeare, Dante Alighieri, Johannes Gutenberg, Galileo Galilei, Nicolaus Copernicus, Christopher Columbus, Vasco da Gama, and Ferdinand Magellan. Science focused on the natural world and the human body with studies in astronomy, physics, navigation, and anatomy. This era laid the foundation for modern science. The conquest to explore the world led to new trade routes and possibilities. Vernacular language emerged in literature at this time as well as the Gutenberg press, making literature more accessible to the general public. Focus shifted from religion to human potential and achievements and individual experience. This was known as humanism. There was a focus on building upon ideas and achievements from antiquity.

## Important notes on the Atlantic Slave Trade

The Atlantic Slave Trade ran between the 15th century - 19th century. Portugal, Spain, England, France, and the Netherlands played major roles in keeping the trade going. African kingdoms including Dahomey, Ashanti, and Kongo were involved in the capture and selling of their African rivals. Many slaves were bought and sold for colonies in the Caribbean, Brazil, and North America for labor. This trade led to depopulation of certain areas within Africa and destabilized traditional economies, fueling more wars between African kingdoms. European nations profited from buying and selling slaves, which helped fuel their global expansion. They also benefited from the slave labor in the production of more goods. Slaves were a crucial force in the development and success in the American colonies as well. Sugar, tobacco, and cotton were central to the global economy. Abolitionists saw slavery as morally wrong and opposed the practice. Heavy abolitionist movements gained momentum in the 18th and 19th centuries. Because of forced migration and the amount of time between capturing and freeing, African slaves stayed in the relocated areas, changing the demographics of the areas they were forced into. African culture melted into and blended with indigenous and European cultures, especially in North America.

## Important notes on the Napoleonic Wars

Napoleon Bonaparte overthrew the French directory in 1799 and declared himself Emperor in 1804, strengthening the central government while reducing the power of nobility. He introduced the Napoleonic code, which were civil codes which gave more equality amongst men (though not so much for women). Before his takeover, France was in a state of revolution. The French Revolution lasted from 1792-1802. It was during this time that Napoleon emerged as a political and military figure. Through the various campaigns, Napoleon revolutionized military tactics by rapidly moving his troops and using artillery. Other nations were forced to match these tactics, modernizing military practices across Europe and leading to larger organized armies. Napoleon spread the idea of legal equality and secular governance. Because of the invasions by France during this period, the European map changed quite a bit and caused nationalism amongst European nations. Innovations in military technologies also resulted. Napoleonic reforms which were based on one's merit and contributions, led to a decline in feudalism across Europe.

## Important notes on 19th Century China

The Qing Dynasty ran from 1644-1912. It was the last imperial dynasty in China. Corruption and ineffective governance were largely to blame for the fall of this dynasty. Bureaucratic inefficiency got in the way of responding to outside challenges. Rapid population growth also outpaced agriculture and economic development. The 18th-19th centuries were marked by civil dissatisfaction and rebellion. War took its toll as well. Reform fell short of modernization.

The first Opium War (1839-1842) were a result of the Qing government attempting to stop illegal opium trade from British merchants for Chinese tea. China faced a large opium addiction problem. In response, Britain retaliated leading to a series of skirmishes. Notable battles include the Battle of the Pearl River Forts and the capture of Nanjing. This war ended with the Treaty of Nanking which did not favor China. This Treaty sparked the Second Opium War (1856-1860). Britain allied with France. Key battles include the capture of Canton and the sacking of the Summer Palace in Beijing. Many important cultural relics were taken. Ultimately, this war ended with the Convention of Peking, where opium trade was legalized. These treaties eroded China's sovereignty and weakened their power. The wars weakened the Qing dynasty.

# History

**Important notes on 19th Century China (continued)**

China was made to repay Western powers as a result of the Opium Wars, further weakening the Chinese economy. Christian missionaries also began causing friction in the nation. Western education and culture began seeping into the nation. There was large effort to modernize China during this period to keep up with the changing world. The Taiping rebellion highlighted this need for reformation. The Taiping Rebellion lasted from 1850-1864 and was one of the biggest and most devastating rebellions in Chinese history. High taxes coupled with widespread poverty and famine fueled the rebellion. Hong Xiuquan led the rebels. The Taiping forces quickly gained followers wishing for social equality and land redistribution. They captured several cities including Nanjing, which became their capital. They implemented radical social reform. The Chinese government used military force against the rebellion. 20-30 million deaths were estimated to come during this period. Internal conflict as well as the exhaustion of resources to the rebellion and attacks from the Qing government eventually ended the rebellion, though much of the Chinese landscape was already devastated.

**Important notes on the fall of the Ottoman Empire**

The Ottoman Empire lasted from the 13th century to the early 20th century. It was founded in 1299 by Osman I in Anatolia. It expanded rapidly through the Balkans and Asia Minor. When it captured Constantinople in 1453, it marked the end of the Byzantine Empire and the beginning of the Ottoman dominance in the area. Under this empire, Islamic law coexisted with secular laws. Th empire began to decline in the late 17th century with military defeat by Russia and European forces, economic stagnation, and internal conflict. The fall of the empire allowed for the emergence of new nation-states in the Middle East. The partitioning of territories did not always align with ethnic and religious demographics, adding to ongoing religious tensions in the area. This era roots conflicts such as Arab nationalism and Arab-Israeli conflicts. This region still struggles with debates over secular and religious governance.

**Important notes on Australia during WWI**

During WWI, Australia was a dominion of the British Empire. Australia aided allied forces during this war. The Australian and New Zealand Army Corps was formed in 1915 to support British operations. In 1915, the ANZAC troops landed in Gallipoli in a campaign against the Ottoman empire, which ended in allied withdrawal. The campaign was disastrous for the allies. Australian forces were also deployed in the battles of Fromelles, Pozieres, Bullecourt, and Passchendaele. They gained a reputation of bravery and resilience in combat. Back home, Australians produced war materials, made recruitment efforts, and kept civilian morale high. Over 60,000 Australians were killed with many more wounded. The war added to Australia's conversations of becoming independent from Britain, changing the ideas the citizens held about their identity as a nation.

**Important notes on the Russian Revolution and Communism**

In the years leading up to the revolution, poverty and harsh working conditions were rampant. The authoritarian rule of Tsar Nicholas II and lack of political reform coupled with suppression of dissent aided in fueling the revolution. A rival party called the Bolsheviks (Led by Vladimir Lenin) seized power in a coup against the government in Petrograd. The Bolshevik party's execution of the Romanov family (Nicholas II and his family) in 1917 symbolized the end of the monarchy and the elimination of the old regime. This led to a Russian civil war between the Bolsheviks and anti-Bolshevik forces. In combination with terrible famine and a harsh winter in 1919-1920, it is estimated that tens of millions of Russians died during the period of the Russian Civil War (1917-1922).

Lenin established a socialist state. Later, the formation of the Union of the Soviet Socialist Republics (USSR) in 1922, established a republic of states under Bolshevik control. This Bolshevik party was later renamed as the Communist Party of the Soviet Union. It was a one-party rule. Communism ideology is based on the writings of Karl Marx and Vladimir Lenin. They advocated for the overthrow of capitalism and the transition to a classless society. Under communism, agricultural lands were seized into state control, eliminating private land ownership in the name of increased production. Censorship and labor camps (gulags) suppressed dissent of citizens. Social upheaval and forced relocation were also markers of the regime. The government moved towards industrialization under Joseph Stalin in an effort to make Russia a world economic power.

# History

**Important notes on the Manhattan Project**

The Manhattan Project was a secret research and development project during WWII which originated out of fear that Nazi Germany was developing nuclear weapons. Albert Einstein warned President Franklin Roosevelt of nuclear fission in 1939. In 1942, the Manhattan project was launched with physicist J. Robert Oppenheimer leading the project. Research and production occurred across the United States in various military facilities. This project led to the successful creation of atomic bombs which were later deployed over the cities of Hiroshima and Nagasaki, Japan in August of 1945. These were the only times nuclear weapons were used in warfare, leading to massive devastation and death among Japanese civilians. These bombings led to Japanese surrender on August 15, 1945, ending the war in the Pacific. The incident ultimately ushered in the age of nuclear weaponry and the Cold War, raising profound ethical questions about their use. Many people involved in the Manhattan Project expressed regret in the creation of nuclear weapons. Oppenheimer later expressed regret in his involvement in the creation of the atomic bomb and advocated against the creation of the hydrogen bomb. Leo Szilard lobbied for control of nuclear energy. Joseph Rotblat left the project and co-founded the Pugwash Conference on Science and World Affairs. Albert Einstein also regretted his indirect involvement in the production of the bomb in his famous letter to President Roosevelt.

**Important notes on the Korean War**

After World War II, Korea was divided along what is called the 38th Parallel. North Korea was controlled by the communist Soviets and South Korea was controlled by capitalist United States. In 1950, North Korea (backed by the Soviets and China) invaded South Korea. Their goal was to reunify the two sides into one communist state. The United Nations forces, in September 1950, led by General Douglas MacArthur, landed at Inchon. They pushed North Korean forces back. After this, China intervened on the side of North Korea, leading to a stalemate at the border. There were many casualties on both sides of the conflict. An armistice was signed in July of 1953 which established a demilitarized zone along the 38th parallel to quell any further conflict. This zone still exists as one of the world's most heavily fortified borders. This became a proxy conflict between the communist and capitalist nations, heightening Cold War tensions. South Korea has become a major technological and economical powerhouse in Asia, while North Korea remains under strict communist control.

**Important notes on the Korean War**

After World War II, Germany was decidedly divided amongst 4 powers (Yalta Conference): the Soviets, United States, Britain, and France. Berlin, the capital, was also split despite being inside Soviet territory. Because of the existing tensions between the Allies and the Soviets, two German states were created in 1949. These were the Federal Republic of Germany, controlled by the Allies (West Germany), and the German Democratic Republic by the Soviets (East Germany). Because West Berlin was thriving under capitalist control, many East Berliners began fleeing to the West side. The East German government constructed a wall to separate the two sides and prevent this from happening. Construction began in 1961. The wall largely symbolized the divide between communist and capitalist worlds - the "Iron Curtain." Families and friends were separated, and lives were disrupted by this wall. An estimated 100-200 people died in the process of attempting to escape over the wall. In 1987, President Ronald Reagan gave his famous speech, imploring Soviet leader Mikhail Gorbachev to "Tear down this wall!" In November of 1989, the German government announced that citizens could cross the border which led to citizens dismantling the wall. This marked the beginning of the end of the Cold War for many.

**Important notes on the Berlin Wall**

After World War II, Germany was decidedly divided amongst 4 powers (Yalta Conference): the Soviets, United States, Britain, and France. Berlin, the capital, was also split despite being inside Soviet territory. Because of the existing tensions between the Allies and the Soviets, two German states were created in 1949. These were the Federal Republic of Germany, controlled by the Allies (West Germany), and the German Democratic Republic by the Soviets (East Germany). Because West Berlin was thriving under capitalist control, many East Berliners began fleeing to the West side. The East German government constructed a wall to separate the two sides and prevent this from happening. Construction began in 1961. The wall largely symbolized the divide between communist and capitalist worlds - the "Iron Curtain." Families and friends were separated, and lives were disrupted by this wall. An estimated 100-200 people died in the process of attempting to escape over the wall. In 1987, President Ronald Reagan gave his famous speech, imploring Soviet leader Mikhail Gorbachev to "Tear down this wall!" In November of 1989, the German government announced that citizens could cross the border which led to citizens dismantling the wall. This marked the beginning of the end of the Cold War for many.

# History

**Important notes on the Space Race**

The Space Race was an event that occurred as a result of tensions between the USSR and the United States after the Second World War, during the Cold War. Its focus was on new achievements in aerospace technologies. The fuel that drove the race was a competition of technology, military power, and ideological differences. Both superpowers sought to show their technological and ideological superiority. The Space Race officially began with the launch of the first artificial satellite by the Soviets called Sputnik on October 4, 1957. This caused the United States to invest heavily in such technologies. Sergei Korolev was an important figure in early Soviet Space Race achievements, while Wernher von Braun, the former German rocket scientist was a leading figure for the Americans. He was instrumental in designing the Saturn V rocket which later powered the Apollo missions. Yuri Gagarin became the first person to orbit Earth on April 12, 1961. He was a Soviet cosmonaut. In 1959, Luna 2 was the first spacecraft to impact the moon. It was launched by the Soviets. And in 1966 they made the first soft landing with Luna 9. In 1961, US President John F. Kennedy challenged the nation to land a man on the moon by the end of the decade. In 1969 America sent the first successful craft to land on the moon with humans Neil Armstrong and Buzz Aldrin. Both the US and the USSR gained public support by boasting their technologies and rallying citizens to support the race to be first. This race led to significant advancements in rocketry, telecommunications, material sciences, and computer technology. Many technologies we use today came from this race including satellite GPS and medical devices. Eventually, the race led to a collaborative effort in space exploration in projects such as the International Space Station.

**Important notes on the Apartheid of South Africa**

The Apartheid of South Africa lasted from 1948 - 1990's. The country of South Africa was colonized by the Dutch in the 1600's and then later by the British in the 1800's. During these periods, indigenous African populations were exploited, and their land and resources were controlled by those who colonized the area. The indigenous people were subjugated and discriminated against by the colonists. The British Parliament passed laws to institutionalize and legalize the apartheid system, which is a system of lawful racial segregation and discrimination. These mew laws classified people by race. This allowed the white European minority to hold power and privilege over the natives and other groups. In 1950, the Population Registration Act required all citizens to be registered as either white, black, colored, or Indian. The Group Areas Act was also passed that year which segregated residential areas by race. Any non-white was forcibly removed from white areas. The African National Congress founded in 1912 was a leading organization in fighting the Apartheid, with Nelson Mandela being a member. He was imprisoned for 27 years for his anti-apartheid activities. Many countries came together to impose sanctions on South Africa for their policies. Many organizations boycotted South Africa to put pressure on the government. The Soweto Uprising in 1976 was a student protest which led to violence and international attention. The release of Nelson Mandela from prison in 1990 marked the beginning of the end of the apartheid. In 1994 he was elected president of South Africa. The Truth and Reconciliation Commission was established to investigate crimes against citizens during the apartheid, which helped uncover the atrocities which occurred and rebuild healing in the nation. South Africa still suffers economic stresses which stem from this period., including high unemployment and poverty. Efforts to improve education and job opportunities for all citizens are ongoing. Educating students about the atrocities of such policies and reinforcing the importance of civil liberties can help prevent this in the future as well as enforcing preventative laws. Racism is still a significant issue in the nation today.

**Important notes on Security After 9/11**

After the Soviet-Afghan War, militant groups began to emerge in the area in and around Afghanistan. One of these groups, al-Qaeda, was co-founded in 1988 by Osama bin Laden. The objective of the organization was to get Western influences out of the region. After Operation Desert Storm (1990-1991) led to US military presence in Saudi Arabia, the US became a larger issue for the organization. The United States failed to accept al-Qaeda as a credible threat to security. In 1993, Ramzi Yousef was part of a bombing at the World Trade Center building. He was associated with al-Qaeda.

On September 11, 2001, a terrorist attack was carried out on the World Trade Center. Nearly 3,000 people were killed with additional victims on the planes the terrorists hijacked and used as weapons against the buildings. This led to an invasion of Afghanistan by the US in Operation Enduring Freedom in October 2001 to dismantle al-Qaeda. In 2003, the United States also invaded Iraq to look for weapons of mass destruction.

**Important notes on Security After 9/1 (continued)**

The terrorist attack on New York City left the world in disbelief. The United States was seen as an untouchable force. Because of this, there was a global increase in security, especially in airports and other transportation modes. Countries increased intelligence sharing. The PATRIOT Act, enacted in October 2001, expanded law enforcement's surveillance and investigative powers to counteract terrorism in the United States. The US also established the Department of Homeland Security in 2002 as well as the Transportation and Security Administration in 2001. In 2013 a whistleblower named Edward Snowden showed that the National Security Agency was collecting massive amounts of data on American citizens, which led to a significant debate over privacy rights within the country. The PATRIOT Act also remains under debate. The USA FREEDOM Act of 2015 was created to try eliminating bulk data collection. These laws continue to be revisited.

# Science

## Page 128

Solution 1:

The cell membrane is vital to allowing nutrients in and allowing waste materials to be left out of the cell while also keeping the structures of the cell in place and blocking unwanted, foreign entities from entering. The cell membrane helps keep homeostasis within the cell. The membrane also helps the cell retain shape and structure and also adhere to other cells to form tissue.

Solution 2:

In order to perform the process of photosynthesis, a plant must have light energy (especially blue and red wavelengths to begin the biochemical reaction), carbon dioxide (collected by the stomata), water (absorbed by the roots and transported to the chloroplasts which is then split providing electrons and protons), and pigments (especially chlorophyll to capture the light energy). The products of photosynthesis are glucose (a simple sugar which acts as an energy source for plants fueling cellular respiration) and oxygen (O2) which is released into the atmosphere.

Solution 3:

In order for a cell to perform cellular respiration, the cell must receive glucose and oxygen. The cell then produces $CO_2$, $H_2O$, and ATP or energy. The stages of cellular respiration include glycolysis (where glucose is broken down in the cytoplasm and pyruvate is released), the Krebs cycle (where high energy electrons are produced in the mitochondria), and oxidative phosphorylation (where energy is released creating an electrochemical gradient and chemosis takes place).

Solution 4:

These are the two most common cells found in living things. They have key differences, though. Prokaryotic cells are much smaller than eukaryotic cells - usually by 100 to 1,000 times smaller - and are therefore much simpler in structure. Unlike the eukaryotic cell, it lacks a defined nucleus. Instead, they have a nucleoid region with a single chromosome containing the DNA. The prokaryotic cell also lacks mitochondria, endoplasmic reticulum, Golgi apparatus, and lysosomes. The next biggest difference is in cell division. The prokaryotic cell goes through a process called fission, while the eukaryotic cell undergoes mitosis and meiosis to reproduce.

# Science

## Page 129

Solution 5:

Mitosis is a process of cell division that produces two identical "daughter" cells that are identical to the parent cell with no genetic variation. The chromosome count remains the same in cells produced by mitosis. There are 5 phases in mitosis -prophase, prometaphase (sometimes not listed), metaphase, anaphase, and telophase.

Meiosis is a form of cell division that occurs in reproductive cells, producing gametes in sexually reproducing organisms. During this division, the chromosome count is reduced by half with genetic variation. Meiosis occurs in two rounds -meiosis I and meiosis II (with 4 stages each) which produces 4 "daughter" cells from the parent cell.

Solution 6:

Mitosis is the process by which the cells in tissue reproduce, therefore replacing damaged or dying cells. These old cells are replaced with new, healthy cells. Nearby healthy cells will undergo mitosis and replace their injured or dying neighbor cells. Different cells have different turnover rates and lifespans, and some will regenerate faster than others. Fibroblasts are cells responsible for wound healing and will undergo mitosis to repair the damaged tissue. Stem cells also play a role in reproducing and repairing tissues.

Solution 7:

Plant cells have a cell wall and therefore hold a fixed shape, whereas the animal cell does not. Plant cells contain chloroplasts so they can perform photosynthesis. Animal cells do not. Animal cells contain centrioles for cell division and plant cells do not. The shape of the mitochondria differs between the cells. Animal cells will contain lysosomes. Plant cells can contain similar structures, but not as commonly. The two cells also store energy differently.

## Page 130

Solution 8:

Deoxyribonucleic acid, or DNA, is a molecule that carries and stores the genetic information (or code) and instructions for the development, function, growth, and reproduction of living things. It is in the form of a double helix structure comprised of two polynucleotide chains held together by hydrogen bonds.

Solutuin 9:

A dominant gene will be expressed phenotypically even if it is present in the heterozygous state (one copy of the dominant allele and one of the recessive). It is often considered "bossy" because when it is present, it is the gene that is seen and the recessive gene is not. Dominant alleles are usually written as uppercase letters. A recessive gene will only be observed in a homozygous state. Recessive alleles are represented by lowercase letters

Solution 10:

DNA (deoxyribonucleic acid) is like the blueprint for building and operating a living thing. It is found inside the nucleus of the cell. RNA (ribonucleic acid) is a messenger for the DNA, helping it perform the instructions of the DNA. It helps carry out tasks dictated by the DNA. There are different types of RNA including messenger (mRNA), transfer (tRNA), and ribosomal (rRNA) which are all produced inside the cell as needed in various locations depending on the type. The structures of the two also differ. DNA is shaped like a double helix, whereas RNA is a single strand.

# Science

## Page 130
Solution 11:

Symbiosis describes the relationship between two organisms living in close proximity to each other. It is usually understood to be mutually beneficial, but it is not always so. Symbiosis can benefit one organism while having a neutral effect on the other. It can also benefit one organism while harming the other. In parasitism the parasite benefits at the expense of the host.

## Page 131
Solution 12:

An animal cell needs water to maintain shape and complete cellular processes, oxygen for aerobic respiration, nutrients including carbs, proteins, and vitamins and minerals, temperature regulation, and waste removal.

Solution 13:

Enzymes are substances (usually proteins) produced by organisms that speed up or act as a catalyst for biochemical reactions. They help in performing cellular processes by lowering the amount of energy the cell needs to complete the process. They can build up or break down other substances. Enzymes can be affected by pH and temperature.

Solution 14:

A macromolecule is a large molecule. It is made of many covalently bonded atoms. Proteins, carbohydrates, and nucleic acids are examples of macromolecules. These are important to the completion of biological processes. Proteins, for example provide structural support to cells, tissues, and organs among other functions.

Solution 15:

A polymer is a large molecule made up of repeating, covalently bonded monomers. Polymerization is the process whereby these monomers are bonded together to form the polymer. The types of polymers include synthetic, natural, and biopolymers. DNA is an example of a polymer.

## Page 132
Solution 16:

Covalent and ionic bonds are both types of chemical bonds. These bonds are the forces holding the atoms inside molecules. Covalent bonds occur between nonmental atoms where they share one or more pairs of electrons. The sharing of the bonds causes a stable electron configuration.

An ionic bond occurs between one metal and one nonmental (usually) atom where one atom gives an electron to the other atom, resulting in either a negatively or positively charged ion.

Solution 17:

An ion is an atom that is either positively or negatively charged because it has either lost or gained an electron. If it has lost an electron, it results in a positive charge. When it gains an electron, it becomes negatively charged. This is because the electrons hold a negative charge. Ionization occurs because of the transfer of electrons between atoms or molecules. Solutions containing ions are called electrolytes. Because they hold the charged ions, electrolytes can conduct electricity.

Solution 18:

Electrolytes help balance blood acidity and pressure by maintaining fluid levels in the body as well as regulating nerve and muscle function.

Made in the USA
Coppell, TX
02 August 2024